A devotional is a tool that we can have and use that will connect us with God and the inner spirit that God wants to touch. These devotions will be a great tool to use in individual quiet times or with groups. The key is that Tom is a vessel that shares from the heart of God ... .

—*Pastor Rod Smith*,
Chippewa UMC,
Beaver Falls, Pennsylvania

Honest, practical, transparent, helpful, insightful; some of the ways Tom Frye's excellent set of daily devotions will strike you. They will help you deepen your companioning worship walk with Jesus. Thank you, Tom.

—*Rev. Dr. Byron Spradlin*,
President, Artists in Christian
Testimony International
Nashville, Tennessee

This devotional is very inspirational. Tom Frye has used real life situations to express Spiritual truth in all 101 writings. These devotions are a great way to be uplifted, convicted and challenged in our everyday Christian life and walk.

—*Jim Stewart*,
NewLife FM Griffin, Georgia

In my sixty plus years on this earth I've literally come in contact with thousands of individuals and only a handful of them stick out for one reason or another. Tom Frye is one of those select few.

I met Tom and his family a few years back thru the recording industry and immediately liked this guy. Tom is the type of person that if every man were honest with himself would love to have as his best friend. His smile is infectious, he has an unshakable love for his wife and children, but most importantly Tom loves Jesus.

Such was not always the case; I know life has not always been easy for Tom and he still has some weeds and thorns in his rose garden of life; then again; don't we all. However with that said; the one poignant, irrefutable, without a doubt certainty is that Tom loves his Savior. When in a conversation with Tom sooner rather than later that conversation will be about Jesus Christ.

I am proud to call Tom my friend and glad to recommend this book of devotions. If you would enjoy a closer walk with God then I would suggest that you spend a few minutes each day walking thru Tom's rose garden by reading 101 Devotions for Busy Families.

—*Bob Horstman*,
WTGN FM, Lima, Ohio

*But seek first His kingdom and His righteousness,
and all these things will be added to you.*

Matthew 6:33 NASB

101

DEVOTIONS FOR

BUSY

FAMILIES

Tom Frye and
The Frye Family Band

Carpenter's Son Publishing

FRANKLIN, TENNESSEE

101 Devotions For Busy Families

Printed in the United States of America

First Printing, 2013

ISBN 978-0-9893722-5-1

Carpenter's Son Publishing
307 Verde Meadow Drive,
Franklin, TN 37067

Layout and design by Eric Shawver, EricShawver.com

Photography by Amy Sprunger of Amy's Photography

Foreword

Family: *an institution, established by God (Genesis 1:27–28), for the purpose of reflecting His personality to those in our home (Ephesians 5:22–6:4), and in which we equip our children to live a life of purpose (Proverbs 1:8-9).*

It is through the love of a husband and wife we, as parents, demonstrate Christ's passion for and devotion to His bride, the church. It is in the "training and instruction of the Lord" (Ephesians 6:4) we model both God's tender mercy and patient nurturing. And by the aforementioned mercy and nurture that our children receive, as an inheritance, the tools necessary to sow into the next generation the abundance of God's blessings.

Tom and Lisa Frye are genuinely inspirational to anyone trying to raise God-centered children. It is clear in spending time with them they have given their art completely to God and in turn God has blessed their efforts. Through their music and ministry, the Fryes are a testament to the blessings we receive when we are willing to live by the values and principles found in scripture.

I am well aware—having three children of my own—that parenting brings with it its share of ups and downs, and I believe whole-heartedly in the necessity of family prayer and devotions to help guide us. This new devotional by Tom and his family will serve as a great compliment to your current family devotions or perhaps as the needed encouragement to begin to make family devotions a regular part of your life together. The stories and observations in the following pages are both inspiring and thought-provoking. Thank you Tom and family for dedicating the necessary time to the writing of this book of devotions, may God multiply His kingdom through your work!

—***Joe Beck,***
writer of over 20 number one songs in both Christian and Country music including Can't Live a Day*

*Connie Rae Harrington and Joe Beck, Avalon:
 In a Different Light (©1999 Bridge Building Music, Universal Music)

Introduction

It is a snowy New Years Eve day, as I wrap up the writing of this devotional. As I reflect on the past nine months of writing and editing followed by more writing, proof-reading and more editing, I am reminded of the hard work and joy it has been to fill these pages and the privilege of being able to do so with my family.

As a songwriter, one of the biggest compliments I can receive is to hear: *I've always felt that, but have never been able to put it into words*. It is altogether humbling to know that something I have written has helped someone else flesh out their faith and I pray the stories in these pages will do the same.

In writing this, my intent has been to honestly share the ways in which I have seen God at work in my own life and in the lives of my friends and family. My hope is that through these stories and observations you will be more aware of God's redemptive work in your own life. And as a result know more fully the love of the Father who sent His only begotten Son into this world—thrown into chaos as a result of sin—not just to provide the means by which we can enter Heaven, but to woo us to Himself.

1 Peter 3:15–16
Tom, on behalf of the Frye Family

Acknowledgments

I enjoy writing: songs, blogs, and now this collection of devotions, but this would have never happened without the help and encouragement of many people, namely our publicist Gina Adams at The Adams Group, who first suggested I write this. My wife Lisa and our children Kaylyn, Maggie and Jonathon, who not only contributed directly to a handful of devotions, but also listened to me as I worked through ideas, helped me edit, and extended to me much needed grace and understanding as I spent many hours during the last nine months of 2012 preoccupied with writing down my thoughts—stealing away for a few minutes to take advantage of a sudden burst of inspiration or sometimes for hours at a time to edit.

I would also like to thank Toni Fennig and Terry Fennig who not only offered their insights but validation. Joe Beck for blessing me with the writing of this foreword, thanks for your encouragement and friendship. So many of our friends and fellow songwriters who encourage and inspire us, including: Mitch McVicker, Jeremy Casella, Andy Osenga, Andy Gullahorn and Jimmy Fortune. And though we never knew him, to Rich Mullins, whose music continues to inspire us. Thanks also to Pastor Darrell Borders and our wonderful church family at Westchester United Methodist Church. To the Fennigs, the Sprungers, the Todds, the Conversets, Eric Shawver, Wendell Gafford of Creative Promotions, Dean and Jennifer Inman, Barry Miller, Steve and Terry Fennig, Jeff and Julie Chrisman, Kevin and Anne Marie Todd, Ron and Loni Freeman, Mary Beth Chapman, John Boggs, Adam Koehler, Pete Peterson, Jim Stewart, Byron Spradlin, Larry Carpenter, Bob Horstman, Pastor Rod Smith, Kevin Culy, Marty Wright, Jim and Phylis Chapman and all the folks at Artists in Christian Testimony and World Vision.

Contents

A life of freedom and purpose 85

About the author 111

Notes 113

Building a legacy of faith

....

These are the commands, decrees and laws the LORD your God directed me to teach you to observe in the land that you are crossing the Jordan to possess, so that you, your children and their children after them may fear the LORD your God as long as you live by keeping all His decrees and commands that I give you, and so that you may enjoy long life.

—Deuteronomy 6:1–2 (NIV)

We pray You'll know them as You knew us when You wove us. As You hold us, hold them, please hold them. Like their father, they are looking for a home, looking for a home beyond the sea. So be their God and guide them till they lie beneath these hills. And let the great God of their father be the great God of my children still.

—Andrew Peterson & Ben Shive
from the song "God of My Fathers"[1]

I am trying here to prevent anyone saying the really foolish thing that people often say about Him: I'm ready to accept Jesus as a great moral teacher, but I don't accept His claim to be God. That is the one thing we must not say. A man who was merely a man and said the sort of things Jesus said would not be a great moral teacher. He would either be a lunatic—on the level with the man who says he is a poached egg—or else he would be the Devil of Hell. You must make your choice. Either this man was, and is, the Son of God, or else a madman or something worse. You can shut Him up for a fool, you can spit at Him and kill Him as a demon or you can fall at His feet and call Him Lord and God, but let us not come with any patronizing nonsense about His being a great human teacher. He has not left that open to us. He did not intend to.

—C.S. Lewis,
Mere Christianity[2]

1

Lessons in every day life

Impress them on your children, talk about them when you sit at home and when you walk along the road, when you lie down and when you get up.

—*Deuteronomy 6:7 NIV*

As I STARTED OUT TO WRITE this devotional, I set a goal of 101 entries. I asked my family to chime in with a few, but promised I would do most of the writing. I started by making a list of ideas: stories I have shared, things I have experienced, Scriptures which have been important to me, and a few song references. Even with all of that to pull from, I was well short of my goal, but as I started writing, I soon found an abundance of inspiration, and it came from everyday life: a conversation with my family during devotions, a friend dealing with loss, gardening—all applicable in pointing to the ever-present God. Soon my challenge was not the lack of material, but rather, which ideas to set aside for another time.

I found myself thankful for this heightened sense of awareness, not only because of the over-abundance of inspiration, but more so for the increased sense of God's presence even during my normal daily routines and responsibilities.

God's presence and faithfulness abound. Sometimes in the hustle and bustle of life it is easy to overlook this truth, but Deuteronomy chapter six implores us to keep it in sight. Doing so affords us many benefits: discipleship, problem solving, and certainly fostering an environment of communication and understanding, all of which are central to having healthy, meaningful relationships with God and family.

Discuss: *Deuteronomy 6*
What do you think it means for *these commands to be upon your hearts*? (v7)
What does it mean to *fear the Lord*? (v13)

Your first ministry

*If anyone does not know how to manage his own family,
how can he take care of God's church?*

—*1 Timothy 3:5 NIV*

MANY YEARS AGO I was approaching burnout. I had recently started a new job in sales and was trying to build my account list. I was in the Optimist Club, sat on the local United Way board, and held too many positions in the small, rural Indiana church in which I was raised. On top of that, Lisa and I were caregivers to my elderly grandmother, and we had two toddlers and a newborn.

One day I was sharing with a friend about my increasing level of burnout. His advice to me marked the beginning of a whole new approach to life. "Tom," he said, "don't forget your family is your first ministry." Wow. There was immediate conviction followed by relief and freedom. For the first time in my life I felt permission to say, "No." I began to work myself out of obligations and make my wife and children the priority they should have been all along. This was hard at first, as I had always been a people-pleaser. I felt both internal and external guilt. I even angered some friends and family members. But what I either gave up or lost in no way compares to the joy I have gained. My wife is honestly my best friend and my children are not just the apples of my eye but my bandmates … how cool is that!?

Don't get me wrong, we have struggles like any other family, but I have come to realize the importance of right priorities.

The right decisions are not always popular, but the benefits they afford are without compare.

Read and discuss: *Daniel 1*

Talk about the decision by Daniel, Hananiah, Mishael and Azariah not to eat the assigned food and drink.

In what ways might you be tempted to compromise your relationship with God and family?

Heavenly lullabies

....

The Lord your God is with you, He is mighty to save.
He will take great delight in you, He will quiet you with His love,
He will rejoice over you with singing.
—Zephaniah 3:17 NIV

WHEN OUR CHILDREN WERE LITTLE, Lisa spent many hours singing softly as she rocked them: "Jesus Loves Me," "I am a Promise," "The B-I-B-L-E," and other children's songs and choruses about God and His love. We often laugh about the time when our son Jonathon reached up with his little hand and covered his mother's mouth, but that did not dissuade her from continuing to sing.

She would sing as they drifted off to sleep, to calm them when they were upset, to comfort them when they were sick, and sometimes just because.

There are few things more intimate than a mother singing over her children as she cradles them in her arms—the love, security, and affirmation afforded a child in those moments can solidify the foundation of a deep and meaningful relationship. But did you know God sings over us, His children, too?

Becoming a parent has helped me to better understand the depths of God's love; a God who loves to see us have fun and enjoy life, to appreciate His creation, to use the gifts He has given us, to live a life of purpose, and when need be, to correct us, not because He enjoys discipline but because He loves.

Most parents would, if need be, lay down their life for their children, but God *did*! Christ's sacrificial death is central to our faith, a truth so familiar we seldom ponder its depth. But have you ever stopped to consider that God not only laid down His life for us, but rejoices over us with singing? That is our Heavenly Father's love: unconditional and complete.

....

Read and discuss: *Zephaniah 3:17, John 3:16* and *Revelation 3:19*

The paint job

....

Fathers, do not exasperate your children; instead,
bring them up in the training and instruction of the Lord.

—Ephesians 6:4 NIV

A FEW YEARS AGO we were painting some cabinets and I asked my son, Jonathon, if he would like to help. He tried to act as if it wasn't a big deal, but I could tell he was tickled. I continued working on something else nearby as two little neighbor boys came up and began talking with Jonathon. They thought it was cool that he was painting, and I could tell their affirmation pleased him. Then it happened. I came over to see how he was doing and I noticed he was painting against the grain, which is not how I wanted it. While I did not go off in a tirade, I did openly voice my frustration, in front of the boys no less, letting him know that I would have to remove the paint and start over. I had just succeeded in squelching my son's spirit and found myself in need of offering an apology.

My response was born out of the wrong assumption that because I knew how I wanted the door painted, my son should automatically have known as well.

As parents we can do the same with our values and faith. We can mistakenly assume that because we hold to certain convictions or make our faith a priority, it will automatically be the same with our children. When we fail to train and instruct our children, we will be prone to (as Ephesians tells us) exasperate them. Values which are not taught, discussed, and lived out are not necessarily valuable to anyone else around us. Discipleship does not happen through osmosis; it takes deliberate effort, patience, and love.

....

Consider:

What values do you wish to pass on to those around you?

Are you making a deliberate effort to make it happen?

A warrior's arrow

....

Like arrows in the hands of a warrior
are children born in one's youth.

—Psalm 127:4 NASB

A YEAR AND A HALF BEFORE we began homeschooling our oldest daughter, Lisa and I attended our first homeschool conference. No one in our family had ever set out on such an adventure, so we were starting from scratch and wanted to give ourselves plenty of time to make the best decision for our family.

Throughout the weekend, Psalm 127:4 was referenced repeatedly and has since been a key verse in our parenting philosophy. Its implications speak volumes. A warrior's arrow is meant for one thing: to be sent into the heat of the battle and pierce the heart of the enemy. As parents, it is easy to yield to the temptation to protect our children, and certainly that is part of our responsibility, but ultimately it is preparation for the battles of life, not safety, which should be the driving force in our parenting decisions.

With this understanding we can most effectively prepare our children for a life of purpose: not stunting but honing, not succumbing to complacency but pressing through trials, not imposing our selfish desires or yielding to theirs but fostering within their hearts an understanding of the amazing purpose for which they have been created.

....

Read and discuss: *Psalm 127*
Consider your purpose as it relates to the arrow.
How are you working to advance the Kingdom?

Gardens

....

... stop and consider God's wonders.
—Job 37:14 NIV

Gardening, like a nice cup of dark, rich coffee, is an acquired taste, and I have acquired a taste for both.

From the time my children were old enough to drop seeds into the ground, they have gardened with us. Back then, it took twice as long with their help as it did without. The work would often come to a complete stop as we enjoyed colorful pebbles, made mud sculptures, and named worms and bugs: those early years in the garden are among my sweetest memories.

There are many scriptural truths which can best be understood in the context of gardening. As we cultivate the soil we can recall the energy lost to the weeds of our life; as we witness the crops come to life, we are able to rejoice in the way God has grown us; in consideration of that ripening fruit, we can think back to God's careful pruning in our own life; with the rain we are reminded of those times when our thirsty soul has cried out to be quenched; and in the harvest we thank Him for the life He gives.

As the children have grown, gardening has continued to inspire many meaningful conversations, often directly related to one of the previously mentioned spiritual principles. After all, life began in a garden, Jesus prayed in a garden, and many of the parables were told using agricultural metaphors.

As I think back to those early years and the innocent wonderment through which my children viewed the world, I realize gardening was not work to them but simply another opportunity to enjoy the small, yet wonderful things of creation: something as adults we often overlook.

....

Consider:
Is there a gardening metaphor which is particularly meaningful to you?

Don't put off until tomorrow

Our days may come to seventy years, or eighty, if our strength endures; yet the best of them are but trouble and sorrow, for they quickly pass, and we fly away.

—*Psalm 90:10 NIV*

EIGHTEEN YEARS AGO TODAY I became a father; it was 11:01pm, fifty-nine minutes before Father's Day. I remember so much about that day and, like most fathers, have so many wonderful memories, not only of those first moments but of the eighteen years since. The one thing I cannot get over is how quickly we have gotten here; I mean, eighteen years—it seems like yesterday.

Time goes by so quickly. When you are twenty, forty seems like a far off country, and it is. At twenty, forty is a lifetime away, but that second twenty years goes by in the blink of an eye. Scripture puts it this way: "What is your life? You are a mist that appears for a little while and then vanishes" (James 4:14).

Not only does the average 78.7 year lifespan of today's U.S. resident go by quickly, but the realization that we are not even guaranteed another day makes each moment precious. There are many things in life requiring our time, and some, though mundane—such as laundry or washing dishes—are truly an important part of serving our families, while others, though often given priority: television, surfing the web, etc., can often serve to distract us from that which is essential to a life of purpose.

The older I get, the more I ask myself, *Is this the most important thing I could be doing right now?* This question reminds me to savor each moment with those I love, even in the midst of the responsibilities I might otherwise consider routine.

Consider:

The breadth of life. Are there things in life you have given a higher priority than God and people?

Are you willing to make the necessary changes to err on the side of love?

Seasons

with Lisa Frye

....

> *... be prepared in season and out of season; correct, rebuke*
> *and encourage with great patience and careful instruction.*
>
> —*2 Timothy 4:2 NIV*

IN INDIANA, WE EXPERIENCE every season. And though it is nice to be able to enjoy a cool dip in the pond on a hot summer day, a backyard bonfire in the crisp fall air, or a winter snowball fight with the family, sometimes in January's bitter cold or July's heat and humidity, it is easy to wish for something else.

At the moment, our family is also experiencing a new season as all three of our children are now teenagers and our son, though be it ever so slightly, is now the tallest person in our home.

It is hard to recognize at first, but as soon as the umbilical chord is cut, our children begin the slow journey toward independence; as such, from our earliest parental moments we are preparing them for life on their own.

As Christians, we know that preparation is about more than just physical provision, teaching them a trade, or giving them an education. Equipping our children is, first and foremost, about nurturing them spiritually. Leading our families in the reading of Scripture, prayer, and the modeling of our beliefs through acts of service. This equipping (discipleship) not only helps our children become increasingly self-reliant, but also evermore dependent on God.

Difficult seasons will come, but these trials provide more than just a few gray hairs—they present teaching opportunities that will not only mold character, but strengthen our relationships, reaping a lifetime of benefits.

....

Read: *2 Timothy 4:1–3*
Talk about the benefits of correcting, rebuking and encouraging with patience and instruction.

Can it wait?

....

And now these three remain: faith, hope and love.
But the greatest of these is love.

—1 Corinthians 13:13 NIV

I CAN, IF I ALLOW MYSELF, be a full-fledged practicing workaholic. There is always so much needing to be done: cut the grass, fix a leaky faucet, change the oil in the car, reply to emails, return phone calls, band practice, and the list goes on.

These things are all important, even necessary, but to have healthy family relationships, it is absolutely essential to prioritize our time wisely. For many years, I allowed stuff, work, and the expectations of others to dictate my time, and as a result, I was not in control of my schedule; it was in control of me.

About the time my oldest daughter turned twelve, the realization hit me: *In that same span of time all three of my beautiful children will likely be out of the house.* As I considered how fast our time had already gone, I was overwhelmed with the realization that the coming years would not slow down. I took a serious look at how I was spending my time and began making some necessary adjustments. I am certainly not about to say I have mastered the balance, but I have learned there is always one more call you can make and one more thing you can check off of your to-do list. Those calls and lists will be there tomorrow, but this will not always be the case with our children.

"Love," as the old adage goes, "is spelled T-I-M-E." Taking that into consideration, the best way I know to love my family is just by experiencing life together: working, playing, studying, serving, or simply relaxing with them are all great ways to invest in our relationships, the dividends of which are immeasurable.

....

Consider:
What does your schedule say about your priorities?
Are there any changes you need to make?

A father's love

....

Yet to all who received Him, to those who believed in His name
He gave the right to become children of God.
—*John 1:12 NIV*

I DO NOT THINK ANYTHING HAS HELPED ME comprehend the depth of God's love more than becoming a father. Unconditional love, desire for fellowship, and a relationship built on trust, are not only attributes of the parent-child relationship - they also reflect God's desire for and feelings toward us.

Throughout much of my life, my understanding of God's love was rooted primarily in fear. During those years, I viewed grace more as an excuse to indulge in sin rather than what it truly is: unmerited favor. While grace is not meant to grant us a sin permit, it does afford us the blessing of consequence without condemnation.

According to 2 Corinthians 5:21, Jesus became sin for us so that we could become *the righteousness of God in Him.* It was love which drove Jesus to the cross and paved the way for those who believe in Him to become children of God.

When I think about the amazing amount of love I have for my children, it is hard to imagine that God could love me more. But, as difficult as it is to comprehend, I know at best my love is but a dim reflection of the perfect love God holds for each of us.

....

Read and discuss: *2 Corinthians 5:17–21*

What do you think it means to be the *righteousness of God*?

Consider the meaning of being both children of God and ambassadors for Christ; how are those titles reflected in our actions?

How can the message of *John 1:12* help us overcome any issues of fear?

Role model

....

> *Come, you children, listen to me; I will teach you*
> *the fear of the LORD.*
>
> —*Psalm 34:11 NASB*

"**P**ARENTING IS NOT FOR WEENIES!" ... so says a friend of ours. And you know what? She's right! Parenting requires self-sacrifice, patience, and time—all of which are born of unconditional love. It is not just planting a seed and hoping it grows—that is just the start. It also requires watering, fertilizing, pruning, and guarding against the predators and parasites, which would, if left to their own devices, destroy our children for the sake of selfish gain.

Even as adult children, we desire the approval of our parents. For some this approval is normal, for others it is altogether foreign, but the importance of involved parents—especially fathers—is made shockingly evident in the following statistics. According to Donald Miller, in his book *Father Fiction*,[3] 94 percent of people in prison are men, of which 85 percent grew up in a fatherless home. So, nearly 80 percent of the prison population could theoretically be cut if fathers were simply involved in the lives of their children. To further emphasize the importance of fathers, here is another statistic for consideration—according to the Baptist Press:[4]

- If a child is the first in their home to become a Christian, 3.5 percent of the time their family will also.
- If a mother is the first to follow Christ, there is a 17 percent likelihood her family will do the same.
- *But if a father first accepts Christ, 94 percent of the time his family will follow him into the Christian faith.*

Parenting is indeed not for weenies and the job we do has staggering ramifications in the lives of our children.

....

Consider:

If you are a parent, are you making time to serve, play, work and pray with your children a priority?

If you are not a parent, is there someone you know in need of a mentor?

Discipline

....

My dear child, don't shrug off God's discipline, but don't be crushed by it either. It's the child He loves that He disciplines; the child He embraces, He also corrects.

—*Hebrews 12:6 The Message*

ONE OF THE MOST DIFFICULT ASPECTS of parenting is discipline. Wanting the best for our children, it is easy to err on the side of sternness and never allow them to experience the blessing of grace in failure. The difficulty of discipline can also lead us to err on the side of grace to the extent we avoid any reasonable consequence altogether.

I believe some of the difficulty though, lies in our lack of distinction between discipline and punishment. Scripture tells us God disciplines those He loves. So, in order to best reflect the personality of God to our children, we need to recognize discipline as a loving response to a less than acceptable action.

Discipline, after all, is simply the means by which we correct not only our children but ourselves. Self discipline drives us to healthy lifestyle decisions, a good work ethic, and stronger relationships; likewise, properly disciplining our children does not drive them away from God but draws them to Him.

On the cross, Christ became the recipient of God's wrath, taking upon Himself the *punishment* for the cumulative sin of mankind. His willingness to be our substitute affords us the opportunity to avoid that which our sin deserves, in exchange for the *discipline* of a gracious and loving Father.

When we properly discipline our children in love, we are effectively guiding them down the path which leads to life, bearing out the truth of Hebrews 12:6.

....

Discuss:
The correlation between discipline and love.

13

Ebenezer

....

> *... Each of you is to take up a stone on his shoulder, according to the number of the tribes of the Israelites, to serve as a sign among you. In the future, when your children ask you, "What do these stones mean?" tell them that the flow of the Jordan was cut off before the ark of the covenant of the Lord. When it crossed the Jordan, the waters of the Jordan were cut off. These stones are to be a memorial to the people of Israel forever.*
>
> *—Joshua 4:5–7 NIV*

ONE OF MY FAVORITE HYMNS is "Come Thou Fount." For years however, because I had no clue what an Ebenezer was, I would omit the second verse when using it as part of a worship service. To me an Ebenezer was nothing more than a mean old man in a Dickens novel.

It was not until a few years ago I discovered the actual meaning of the word. An Ebenezer is simply an alter built to commemorate a specific event, as referenced in today's verse. The Ebenezer served as a reminder to future generations of God's faithfulness to His people.

Today we do not typically pile up stones to commemorate God's faithfulness, but we do still honor the tradition of the Ebenezer. Diplomas we hang on the wall, journals we keep, our wedding pictures reminding us not only of the blessing of a spouse but also of the commitment we made before God and family; even our scars can serve as a reminder of God's healing in our lives.

....

Exercise:
List the times in your life when God was very real.
What are some of the Ebenezers that remind you of these events?

Character

....

He who walks in integrity walks securely …
—*Proverbs 10:9 NASB*

WHEN THE KIDS WERE YOUNGER, our family enjoyed many hours of out-loud reading. *The Chronicles of Narnia, Little House on the Prairie* and the lesser known, but equally enjoyable series, *Little Britches*. The latter, written by Ralph Moody, details the early years of the author's life, including his family's move to and from Colorado in the early years of the twentieth century.

There are many wonderful life lessons found in this series, not the least of which is that of the *Character House*.[5] This story communicates clearly how our character is the cumulative total of all our decisions. With each good decision, we help construct our Character House, and with each bad one we tear it down.

It is easy to put off difficult decisions, avoid situations which can potentially bring conflict, or ignore the proverbial elephant in the room, but good character requires we handle each circumstance appropriately. Poor character, after all, is not only made up of bad decisions but of good decisions left undone.

When viewing our life and the lives of our children in this light, we see more clearly the necessity of making the most of every teachable moment. Maybe this requires denying ourselves that extra piece of pie to share with someone else, excusing ourselves in order to discipline our child rather than ignoring or laughing off their public offense, or stopping in the rain to help a stranger change a flat tire. Whatever the case, the character we model and that which we expect from our children will go a long way in helping each of us reflect the love of Christ.

....

Consider:

Are you familiar with the term *Character House*?

How might considering and applying its principles bring an increased sense of peace and purpose?

Exercise

....

*If anyone would come after Me, he must deny himself
and take up his cross daily and follow Me.*

—*Luke 9:23 ESV*

I WAS THINKING TODAY, as I was out for my morning jog, exercise is a lot like love. This may seem like a stretch, but hang in there with me. The word love conjures up many images: from chocolate Valentines to wedding ceremonies, grandma's hugs or our first pet, but love is so much more. "Love is ..." as the adage goes "... a decision," and while we may say "I love you," it is our actions which give our words meaning.

In the same way, one day of exercise will not have lasting results, neither can we expect others to know our true feelings without regularly communicating and, more importantly, demonstrating love. Love modeled through commitment is what motivates us to get out of bed in the middle of the night to comfort a sick child, take a meal to an elderly neighbor, or provide free baby sitting for a single mom so that she can run errands or maybe just take a nap.

It was perhaps this same sentiment which inspired the poet Rainer Maria Rilke[6] to write, "For one human being to love another; that is perhaps the most difficult of all our tasks, the ultimate, the last test and proof, the work for which all other work is but preparation."

....

Consider: *John 15:13* and *Luke 9:23*
What do these verses say about love?

Choose this day

....

> *... choose for yourselves this day whom you will serve, ...*
> *... as for me and my household we will serve the Lord.*
> —*Joshua 24:15 NIV*

THERE ARE TIMES IN OUR LIVES when we reach an impasse, and thus are forced to make a decision, many times knowing full well our lives will forever be changed. These choices can seem as though they must be made in an instant, but in reality they likely represent months, if not years, of preparation.

Before Joshua died, he called the children of Israel together to renew their covenant with God. He recounted how their forefathers, including Terah the father of Abraham, had worshipped other gods. He reminded them of their captivity in Egypt, God's faithfulness in leading them to the Promised Land and the victories won over its inhabitants. He then gave them the opportunity to renew their covenant with God or choose the gods of their forefathers or of the Amorites.

Sometimes false gods can appear quite enticing, appealing to our selfishness, and exploiting our vulnerabilities. Often, it is easier to cling to destructive allegiances and, in blind faith, toe the party line rather than consider another way. But unwillingness to set aside pride and loyalties keep us from objectively weighing our options and hinder us from seeing the truth, greatly increasing the likelihood of poor decisions.

Joshua challenged the people to turn away from the deceptive allure of false gods and, remembering God's faithfulness, renew their covenant with the One True God. This was not a snap decision based on recent history or fleeting passions, but one which resulted from seeing first hand God's faithfulness and experiencing the blessings enjoyed as a result of trusting Him.

....

Read and discuss: *Joshua 24*
What tempts you to turn from God?

The danger of the familiar

It is of the Lord's mercies that we are not consumed,
because His compassions fail not. They are new every morning;
great is Thy faithfulness.

—Lamentations 3:22–23 KJV

I HAVE AN OLD SHIRT that should have been thrown away years ago. It has bleached spots, a few small holes, and the collar is stretched out. I would never wear it in public, but it sure is nice on one of those all too infrequent lounge-around-the-house days. There is just something truly comfortable about the familiar.

Some of my songs are much the same. I have performed them for so long they are almost like old friends. There is a point, however, at which a song can become too familiar. A new song requires extra focus, but when singing an old standby, if I am not careful, I can find myself somewhere in the middle of it wondering, *Is it time for the bridge or the second verse?*

While it is one thing to lose our place in a song, it is quite another to allow relationships to become so familiar we begin to go through the motions without considering how important they are to us. When we flippantly read over Scripture instead of meditating on it as if it were the source of our next breath, when we casually wave goodbye to our children as they go out the door, half heartedly mumble "I love you" to our spouse as we drift off to sleep, or neglect friends for months at a time, we may just be a little too comfortable.

There is nothing like having people in our lives who love us just the way we are, without pretense or condition; who, whether they know it or not, are modeling God's love to us. Much like that old shirt, they are always a comfort—*new every morning*—a love like that we should never take for granted.

Consider:
Can you more effectively model your love to others?

18

Who completes you?

....

... we know and rely on the love God has for us ...
love is made complete among us so that we will have confidence
on the day of judgment ...

—1 John 4:16–17 NIV

I SAW THE MOVIE *JERRY MAGUIRE*[7] years ago. In it, Tom Cruise plays a sports agent who, in the movie's most memorable scene, makes an emotionally charged plea to his wife, whose affection he is trying to recapture. With great passion he declares, "You complete me." While this makes for a great movie and tugs at the heart strings of the viewer, this is not the way it is supposed to be.

I have observed relationships where, in some form or fashion, one individual—who may be very well intended—exacts undue pressure on the other. This can happen among friends, coworkers, board members, in churches, civic organizations, and in families. But I believe this most frequently occurs within the context of marriage.

I am blessed with a wonderful wife. We compliment each other very well; her strengths are my weaknesses and vice-versa. I love her more than anyone in the world, but she does not complete me, nor I her; we can't. The only relationship in which we are able to find true completeness is in our relationship with Christ.

When a spouse attempts to complete the marriage relationship, they unwittingly undertake the impossible task of trying to live up to the role only intended for Jesus. For this reason, their efforts always fall short and serve only to further exaggerate the void and exasperate the relationship. When, however, we find completeness in Jesus, not only our marriages, but all of our relationships will benefit.

....

Read and discuss: *1 John 4:7–21*
Discuss the attributes of perfect love.
Is this reflected in your relationships?

19

A husband's love

....

Husbands, love your wives, just as Christ loved the church
and gave Himself up for her to make her holy, cleansing her
by the washing with water through the word, and to present her
to Himself as a radiant church, without stain or wrinkle or any
other blemish, but holy and blameless.

—*Ephesians 5:25–27 NIV*

WHILE FATHERHOOD HAS HELPED ME better understand God's love, marriage has helped me wrap my mind around the necessity of Jesus' sacrifice, which makes knowing His love possible.

While I am truly blessed with a wonderful marriage, I know, for both of us, marriage takes work: sacrifice, patience, and understanding. Not because we are extra difficult people but simply because we are human and as such predisposed to selfishness. Christ's example, however, provides for us a wholly unselfish model, and the more we learn to imitate His love, the stronger all our relationships will become.

While I do not begin to claim total comprehension of the implications or privileges afforded us by Christ's sacrificial death, I do know the more I put others needs above my own, the more fully I am able to identify with His love, resulting in a greater motivation to serve others.

So how can we see our spouse and others as radiant, without stain, wrinkle, or blemish? By modeling Jesus' limitless love, a love which freely chooses to give up rights and privilege to bear our offense, making fellowship with Him possible.

....

Consider:

Is there any offense you hold to which hinders you from seeing your spouse or others as radiant and without blemish?

If so, consider how Jesus' example might encourage you to give up your right to that offense and in so doing more effectively foreshadow the love of the True Bridegroom to those around us.

Strong character and tender hearts

....

Blessed are the pure in heart, for they will see God.

—Matthew 5:8 NIV

*When wealth is lost, nothing is lost; when health is lost,
something is lost; when character is lost, all is lost.*

—Billy Graham[8]

*Deep down we usually know exactly what the right thing
to do is in any situation. But if we simply don't want to do it,
we won't have any trouble coming up with an endless list of
lame excuses to justify not doing it. In fact, some of the excuses
may even seem like really good ones. Do the right thing anyway.
That's what saints are made from.*

—Mother Teresa[9]

You be Jesus

....

Be imitators of me, as I am of Christ.
—*1 Corinthians 11:1 ESV*

WHEN PREPARING A SNACK for her grandsons, a friend of mine told me she was always careful to give an equal portion to both.

Once, as she was dividing a candy bar, one of the boys noticed the halves were not quite equal. The grandmother, trying to make the most of this teachable moment, told the more vocal of the two, "Jesus would gladly give the bigger portion to his brother." To which, without missing a beat, he replied, "OK, let him be Jesus."

We all have probably felt this way at one time or another. Dying to ourselves and serving others is anything but natural. Whether taking the smaller piece of candy, losing sleep to sit up with a sick child, or helping a stranded stranger change a flat tire, our flesh will always err on the side of selfishness.

Throughout Scripture, we are exhorted to die to our self and to follow the example of Christ. In Ephesians 5:1–2, the apostle Paul encourages us to, "… be imitators of God, as beloved children; and walk in love, just as Christ also loved you and gave Himself up for us, an offering and a sacrifice to God as a fragrant aroma." And in Matthew 16:24–25, Jesus tells us, "If anyone wishes to come after Me, he must deny himself, and take up his cross and follow Me. For whoever wishes to save his life will lose it; but whoever loses his life for My sake will find it …"

Self sacrifice is not easy, but it results in life and peace.

....

Read and discuss: *Galatians 2:20* **and the Scripture above.**

Share about a time when you had to die to yourself.

Honestly discuss the struggle to deny temporary desires for the greater good.

For additional consideration, discuss *2 Corinthians 4:10–12* and *2 Corinthians 4:16–17*.

T.C. Steele

A sluggard's appetite is never filled,
but the desires of the diligent are fully satisfied.

—*Proverbs 13:4 NIV*

SEVERAL YEARS AGO, our family visited the home of world renowned impressionist painter, T.C. Steele. Steele, who was from Indiana, gained international prestige for his paintings of landscapes. However, as we were touring his studio we saw noticeably more portraits displayed among his work. When asked the reason for this disparity, the tour guide informed us that while landscapes were Steele's passion, the portraits paid the bills. I found this information quite inspiring.

I have known people over the years who have given up on their dreams—maybe because they believe the necessary work to be too difficult or perhaps they depend too much on their natural abilities. It is also possible that they have yielded to the temptation to allow society to define their success, failing to realize that when we seek the world's validation and thereby yoke ourselves with the burden of their version of success, we sell ourselves and our dreams short.

When we are unwilling to do the necessary work to maximize our potential we are confessing a greater desire for comfort than for purpose, and in so doing overlook the importance of stewardship as it relates to our giftings.

While we often celebrate those who, like Steele, are willing to do what is necessary to realize their dreams, many times we are prone to simply stand in the gallery of life and marvel at their talents, while neglecting our own. However, if painting portraits is a requirement to achieving our God-given desires, let us be workmen worthy not only of our wages, but also of our dreams.

Consider:
Are you using your passions to serve God and others?

The best policy

....

An honest answer is like a kiss on the lips.
—*Proverbs 24:26 NIV*

IN LIFE, WE ARE PRESENTED with a lot of tough questions; some we do not know how to answer, and others we would just rather avoid altogether. Because of that, we may do our best to ignore the question, and if that doesn't work it can be oh, so tempting to bypass the truth and simply say whatever is most convenient at the moment, whether it is truthful or not. But, a lie is a lie no matter how well intentioned, and shirking a difficult situation only serves to exasperate those involved while, at the same time, compounding the problem.

Culturally, so-called *little white lies* are acceptable. Though often justified through intent, these slight fabrications are lies nonetheless. Often, because of their societal acceptance or intent, these seemingly harmless offences are brushed off as no big deal, but they can set a harmful precedent.

Our children often present us with tough questions, and to avoid the awkwardness of the moment, we can create some very tall tales (storks and cabbage patches come to mind). The key to effectively answering tough questions however, is to give an honest, age-appropriate response. Many times full disclosure would only serve to confuse, frustrate, or mortify our children. Simple honesty, however, satisfies curiosities and reinforces trust.

Honesty and sensitivity flow from love, and are the pillars on which trust is built. Many faults can be tolerated or worked through, but in the absence of honesty there is no solid foundation on which a relationship can stand.

....

Read: *Psalm 15*
What does this Psalm have to say about honesty?
Are there times in your life when you are tempted to be dishonest?
What can you do to overcome these struggles?

The tree

....

... give thanks in all circumstances ...

—*1 Thessalonians 5:18 NIV*

Today is Sunday. This was the weekend I planned to paint my shed. Instead, I spent Friday evening and all day Saturday, in the ninety-plus degree heat, cleaning up from a storm which toppled one of my favorite trees (of course the tree I had planned to cut down later this summer withstood the winds) and cut off power, water, and phone service to our home.

As I began to realize my weekend was slipping away with no hope of cracking open a can of paint, I felt the makings of a pity party beginning to brew. Then I remembered our time in southern Indiana, cleaning up debris and cutting up scores of downed trees left in the wake of a series of tornados which struck Indiana, Kentucky, and Tennessee earlier this year. To further aide in my reality check, I was reminded of the ministry of World Vision, the children we sponsor, and those we have seen sponsored at our concerts. As I thought about their lack of even basic needs, which require many children to walk several miles each day just to fill water containers, my sulking quickly gave way to gratitude.

My setbacks are nothing more than inconveniences, and my frustrations mere selfishness in light of what many experience. When I stop to consider others, it serves to remind me of the amazing blessings I have, and the responsibility I bear to use those blessings for the benefit of the Kingdom.

If you have never gone on a mission trip, I would encourage you to do so; if you have never looked into child sponsorship* I would love for you to consider that as well. Both are wonderful ways to bless others and grow your faith.

....

Consider:
What makes you stop and count your blessings?
*For more information visit **WorldVision.FryeFamilyBand.net**.

The tree II

....

> *Do not boast about tomorrow,*
> *for you do not know what a day may bring forth.*
> **—Proverbs 27:1 NASB**

I TEND TO BE A PLANNER, and as such, though I try, I am prone to allow disruptions to hijack my attitude. The fallen tree mentioned previously not only rerouted my weekend plans, knocked out our power, and afforded me a much needed reality check, but it did something else. It reminded me of the brevity of life.

In the midst of my attitude adjustment, I was reminded of James 4:13–17, which says in part, "… you do not even know what will happen tomorrow. What is your life? You are a mist that appears for a little while and then vanishes."

Life not only goes by quickly, but it can be over in an instant. Had our tree fallen in any other direction, the outcome could have been much worse. While the storm caused a few days of inconvenience for us, it claimed the lives of at least nine people. What was for me nothing more than a weekend of unexpected aggravation, was for others one filled with devastating loss. The reality of life's uncertainty should serve to remind us of the importance of making the most of every moment, taking time to enjoy our blessings in the good times, and count them in the bad. Scripture reminds us in Matthew 5:45, "[God] sends the rain on the righteous and the unrighteous." How we choose to respond to adversity not only says a lot about where our trust lies, but when taken in stride, it can also serve as an amazing testimony to our faith.

....

Read and discuss: *James 4:13–17*
What distracts you from keeping a right perspective?

Can you think of someone who has maintained a good outlook
in spite of bad circumstances?

How has their attitude inspired you?

Every day is a good day if you live to see it

This is the day the Lord has made; let us rejoice and be glad in it

—*Psalm 118:24 ESV*

A S A TEENAGER, I attended the birthday party of an older gentleman in our community. He was well into his 80s and alone, so some of the people from the area decided to throw him a birthday party. I don't even remember his name, but I remember something he said to me that day. I told him I hoped he had a good birthday, to which he replied, "Every day is a good day if you live to see it." This man was elderly; he had experienced the loss of most of his friends and immediate family, yet he was able to say every day is good.

Have you ever heard the saying you can either look at life as a half full or half empty glass? Each day brings opportunity for both sorrow and joy; how we react depends a lot more on our attitude than on the situations around us.

Our attitude can affect our health, our relationships, and certainly our Christian witness. I have known people who, though having seemingly everything, are seldom happy, while others, who have suffered tremendous loss, are still able to smile.

Scripture instructs us, "Be joyful always; pray continually; give thanks in all circumstances, for this is God's will for you in Christ Jesus" (1 Thessalonians 5:16–18). Sometimes a good attitude is a sacrifice and a happy heart is often more about the choice than the circumstance. This sentiment was also shared by the Psalmist when he wrote, "Let them sacrifice thank offerings and tell of His works with songs of joy" (Psalm 107:22).

Discuss:

Are there areas in which you struggle to have a good attitude?

How does our outlook affect our ability to communicate God's love to others?

We're just happy people

Maggie Frye

....

> *A happy heart makes the face cheerful,*
> *but heartache crushes the spirit.*
>
> —*Proverbs 15:13 NIV*

As we approached the checkout counter at the grocery store recently, Mom and I were greeted with a strange question: "What?" The young woman behind the counter, probably in her late twenties, seemed paranoid about something we could not place. We looked at her, at each other, and finally back at her—now obviously confused. She evidently noticed and half asked, "You were both … smiling." Still waiting for an answer, she curiously stared at Mom and me. Laughing, I replied, "I guess we were, weren't we?" Then Mom answered, "Evidently we're just happy people."

Scripture tells us, "A happy heart makes the face cheerful."

In a world that says our very existence is merely a cosmic accident, the idea of hope can seem nothing more than a fairy tale. In our fast-paced, self-focused society, a smile—a seemingly insignificant expression of joy—can be a much needed means of encouragement.

Witnessing for Christ is not always about handing out a tract or even speaking a single word. Sometimes just offering a smile to a stranger or extending grace to the cashier who just miscounted our change can be our most effective form of witness.

Scripture tells us, "the joy of the LORD is your strength" (Nehemiah 8:10). I believe this could speak not only to our stamina or motivation, but also directly to our Christian witness.

....

Consider:

What does our response to those we come in contact with say about our relationship with God?

Create in me a pure heart

*Create in me a pure heart, O God
and renew a steadfast spirit within me.*

—Psalm 51:10 NIV

THE HEART IS PARTICULARLY IMPORTANT TO GOD. Our heart determines so much about our lives, our character, our motives, our attitude, and how we relate to people and to God.

Throughout Scripture we are told to keep God's word in our heart, seek God with all our heart, and love God with all our heart … but why? As our heart goes, so goes the rest of us, body and soul. Our heart defines who we are.

When we hold knowledge only in our head we can easily regurgitate facts without ever having to really understand what we are saying. To put it another way, head knowledge provides a false sense of security which can be quite dangerous to ourselves and those around us, but when we hold knowledge in our hearts, we own it—it will lead and guide us and benefit both others and ourselves.

But there is more. Scripture makes it clear God will give us over to the desires of our heart—good and evil desires alike. In Psalm 37:4, we are told when we delight ourselves in the Lord, He will give us the desires of our heart, which, of course is a positive, but Psalm 81:11–12 reflects a contrasting truth, "But My people would not listen to Me; Israel would not submit to Me. So I gave them over to their stubborn hearts to follow their own devices."

David knew the importance of having a right heart before God. He had fallen so far when he penned the words of Psalm 51 and knew the only way back was through a repentant heart fully surrendered to God.

Read and discuss: *Psalm 51*
For additional discussion consider also *Matthew 12:34*, *Psalm 81*, and *Romans 1:24*.

Don't want to lose the eternal

… love covers a multitude of sins.

—1 Peter 4:8 NLT

ONE OF THE INCREDIBLE BLESSINGS of being involved in music ministry is the opportunity to meet so many wonderful people. While I remember scores of conversations, there is one particular visit with pastor Tom Camp and his wife Terri, which stands out.

Their church is vibrant and growing, full of people from all walks of life; many of whom have come out of lives of abuse, crime, and addiction, but through love, patience, and deliberate discipleship, their lives have been transformed.

After listening to their story over lunch, the reason for this couple's compassion was clear. In their early years, they were also rebels. Looking for answers, Terri began attending a church and soon wanted her future husband to join her; he agreed. However, Tom's first visit to the church was anything but forgettable; he showed up late … and drunk.

Stumbling over each pew, Tom made his way to the front of the church. This blatant irreverence would have been enough to send many churchgoers over the edge, but Tom was met not with condemnation, but love. One elder who willingly looked beyond the moment not only changed the course of Tom and Terri's lives, but also the lives of many others who now sit under their leadership, including Tom and Terri's son, Jeremy, whose songs have ministered to countless people throughout the world.

I am reminded of another Indiana songwriter, Rich Mullins, who in his song "My One Thing" sang, "don't want to lose the eternal for the things that are passing,"[10] a sentiment certainly shared by this patient elder and his protégé.

Read and discuss: *1 Peter 4:7–9*
How does this text apply to the story above?
What can be learned from this couple's story?

Make your bed!

....

Well done, good and faithful servant! You have been faithful with a few things; I will put you in charge of many things. Come and share your master's happiness!

—Matthew 25:23 NIV

WHEN I WAS IN COLLEGE, I had a roommate who made his bed every morning, which admittedly is pretty rare for a college-age male. He always said, "When we are faithful in small things, we will be faithful in big ones as well." He believed making his bed set a good precedent for meeting whatever challenges the day might bring.

The small things are important for many reasons. In the small things we learn the fundamentals, build our strength, and unlock our passions. In the small things we learn patience, humility, perseverance, and the discipline of denying our flesh and facing our fears.

In theater the saying goes, "There are no small parts, only small people." Every part is essential to the telling of the story, and as my children, who have been involved in numerous theatrical productions, will attest: the smaller the part the more difficult the performance. For some, this may be an ego thing, but for most it is simply a matter of the difficulty of getting into character for a short amount of time.

It is natural to overlook or dismiss the small things as insignificant or inconsequential, but our willingness to embrace them says a lot about our character. By avoiding the small things, we may in fact be denying ourselves the very tools necessary to unlock our full potential.

....

Read and discuss:

The parable of the talents in *Matthew 25:14–30*.

What does this say about the importance of the little things?

What is right?

Jonathon Frye

....

> *If anyone, then, knows the good they ought to do*
> *and doesn't do it, it is sin for them.*
>
> —*James 4:17 NIV*

OUR HOUSE IS LOCATED along the Wabash River in rural Indiana. Sometimes, after a heavy rain or a rapid snow melt, the river spills over its banks and covers the roads near our home.

On one of these days, after a heavy snow melt, Maggie decided to go for a walk, but a few minutes later she came rushing back into the house and said, "There's a man stuck in the water!"

We all ran outside to see if we could help. We saw the man, an Amish, whose buggy had been swept off the road by the cold February flood-waters. He was calling out for help as he stood on his horse's back—clinging to a telephone pole.

The neighbors had already called 911, but as we waited for the first responders, it was obvious the situation was growing critical. The first officers soon arrived—without a boat. We continued to wait, but the horse—which was only able to hold its head out of the frigid water—began to grow weak. Just then, Dad saw our neighbor's small flat-bottom boat, which was sitting on a trailer in about two feet of water. As he went in after the boat, I remembered a pair of oars, which belonged to my great-grandpa, hanging in our garage, but getting them required I also wade through the icy flood-waters. As my feet touched the water, I turned back, but as I thought about the man, I knew I had to help. I retrieved the oars and soon the man and his horse were rescued.

My temporary discomfort was soon replaced by the satisfaction of knowing I was able to help. Many times the right thing to do is also the most difficult. But as Scripture reminds us, when we are unwilling to do the right thing, it is sin.

....

Discuss:

Sin as described in *James 4:17*.

The formula for success

As obedient children, do not conform to the evil desires you had when you lived in ignorance.

—*1 Peter 1:14 NIV*

SEVERAL YEARS AGO, when my music ministry was just beginning, I would take any available opportunity to talk with other artists, especially those I perceived as successful. I would ask them all the same question: "How did you get started in music?" Of course I was looking for a formula, a check list, something I could do to become "successful," but I always received the same reply: "I don't know."

There are stories throughout the Bible of God doing miraculous things: winning battles for the children of Israel, healing the blind, and parting the waters, just to name a few. But God rarely did it the same way twice. The Israelites marched around Jericho, blew their trumpets, and the walls came down; they never fought a battle in the same way again. And in Numbers chapter twenty we find the account of Moses' disobedience. What did he do? He tried to follow a formula—striking a rock to receive water—as he had done previously, instead of speaking to it as God had instructed. I can imagine Moses thinking, *You asked me to hit the rock before and it worked.* Maybe he would have felt odd speaking to a rock, maybe he just desired consistency, but while God did honor Moses by providing water, He also punished him by not allowing Moses to lead his people into the Promised Land.

We are creatures of habit, which makes consistency so appealing, but since those early days of ministry, I have come to realize, in music and in life, there is only one clear-cut formula for success: obedience. It is always wise to receive council, but it is never advisable to put more trust in a formula than in God.

Read and discuss: *1 Peter 1:13–25*

33

Failure

....

> *... we know that suffering produces perseverance; perseverance*
> *character; and character, hope. And hope does not disappoint us,*
> *because God has poured out His love into our hearts by the Holy*
> *Spirit, whom He has given us.*
>
> —Romans 5:3–5 NIV

OTHER THAN DUCT TAPE, WD-40 has got to be the most essential product in any man's garage. But had it not been for the perseverance of its inventor, we would have never known the benefits of this multi-faceted product. *WD* stands for Water Displacement and the number 40 is in reference to the fortieth attempt at its creation. When asked about his failures, I have heard it said, inventor John Barry responded, "I didn't fail 39 times, I just learned 39 ways not to make it."

I am a firm believer failure has a lot less to do with an outcome and a lot more to do with our willingness to learn. It is often tempting to play it safe, easy to believe a lie, and considered normal to choose the status quo over the risk of falling flat on our face. But great things are never achieved by simply waiting for lady luck to smile down on us.

As the old adage goes, "It's better to have tried and failed than to have never tried at all." The key is not perfection, but perspective. Failure turned inward breeds self-pity and low self-esteem; failure, viewed properly provides us with powerful life lessons and tremendous opportunities for growth. Perseverance is essential to growth and the willingness to learn a must for success.

....

Read and discuss: *Romans 5:1–11 and James 1:2–16*

What role has perseverance played in your life?

Can you think of a time when you have learned from, or have been motivated by your failings?

How can perseverance shape our character?

What are you saying?

....

... let us not love with word or with tongue,
but in deed and truth.

—*1 John 3:18 NASB*

THERE ARE FEW THINGS I ENJOY more than the challenge of crafting words. Whether it is the poetic nature of songwriting, blogging on my website, or journaling my thoughts for this devotional, writing is something I truly love. Inspiration comes from many places, but for me, I have found I am best able to communicate God's truth through the lens of my own story—remembering a particular event or simply expressing the joys found in our daily routines.

I also appreciate quite an eclectic group of authors and songwriters, each of whom possess the ability to challenge with words both poetic and piercing. Whether communicating their stories with refreshing transparency or sharing God's truth through metaphors both rich and deep, their words have stirred within me a greater hunger for the things of God, inspiring me to press on—even during the most troubling times.

Though most are not writers, everyone communicates something. And in the end it is not the words spoken or the poems penned but actions and deeds, born of love, which accomplish the greater good.

I recently read a quote from the poet Maya Angelou,[11] which sums this up quite nicely: "People will forget what you said, People will forget what you did, But they will never forget how you made them feel!"

Words are important, but when not affirmed through action, they are but a hollow promise communicating nothing more than awareness without conviction.

....

Read and discuss: *1 John 3:17–19 & James 4:17*
What do our actions communicate about our convictions?

What offends you?

....

[Jesus came] to seek and to save the lost.
—*Luke 19:10 ESV*

WHEN I WAS YOUNG, I truly believed God was just waiting for me to step out of line so He could pulverize me. Not only that, but I also knew if I did somehow manage to make it through the day, without being blasted into oblivion, only to die in my sleep without saying my prayers, I would wake up in Hell. It seemed almost everything was "against my religin," including rock and roll, which I was sure would rot my brain.

Fast forward thirty years. Recently my family watched a movie, which, for the most part, was nothing short of one long expletive, interrupted only by the occasional innuendo. Though it was tempting to revert back to those old days of fear and offense and stop the movie midstream, I chose instead a different response. Following the movie, we discussed the language, joking, and hopelessness reflected in the actions of the characters and, though fictitious, how the movie provided a sad glimpse into a life many know as normal. We also discussed the fact that in life, grabbing the remote and pushing stop is not always an option.

Living in this world, we sometimes get blindsided by that which we find offensive, but I think the Kingdom is better served when we choose to look beyond our personal comforts and instead meet people where they are, resolving to allow the hopelessness of the lost to be a call to action and not cause for retreat.

....

Discuss:

Jesus never seemed to be offended when the world acted like the world; instead, He willingly went into the streets to draw *offensive people* to Himself.

How might we do a better job of setting aside our offense in order to bring the love of Christ to the lost?

What are you willing to do to make it happen?

Disposable society

*"Which of these three do you think proved to be a neighbor
to the man who fell into the robbers' hands?" And he said,
"The one who showed mercy toward him." Then Jesus said to
him, "Go and do the same."*

—Luke 10:36–37 NAS

IT SEEMS NOTHING IS MADE TO LAST. We use disposable razors, though increasingly rare, some still use disposable cameras, and when our children were babies, I was certainly thankful for disposable diapers.

Even our major purchases, including vehicles and appliances are built with planned obsolescence in mind. Ultimately though, no matter how well made, all the aforementioned items will someday break, rust, or rot. There is, however, something our society often undervalues, which is altogether eternal: Life.

While listening to the news a few years ago, I was saddened to hear the report of a woman on the edge of a bridge in a busy metropolitan thoroughfare. As she stood there contemplating suicide, angry motorists stuck in the ensuing traffic jam—more concerned about their schedules than the life of this desperate woman—began urging her to jump.

While this lady's life may have been of little or no value to the commuters, her life was of great value to God. So much so that He sent His Son to give His life as a ransom for her own. Often now, when I am tempted to be short with someone in line at the grocery, the waitress who is slow to bring my meal, or the customer service representative whose only job may be simply to fix someone else's mistake, I recall the story of the desperate lady on the bridge and am reminded of the great value of life.

Consider:
How might remembering the lady on the bridge help you better reflect the hope of the Gospel to those you meet?

The reverse pendulum

....

> *For the LORD gives wisdom; From His mouth comes knowledge*
> *and understanding. He stores up sound wisdom for the upright;*
> *He is a shield to those who walk in integrity.*
>
> —*Proverbs 2:6–7 NAS*

I HAVE OFTEN LAMENTED—maybe you have too—about the social, religious and political pendulums prone to swing from one extreme to the other. I have often wondered, *Why can't the pendulum just stop in the middle and afford us all some much needed balance?* But recently I had a conversation which gave me a different perspective on the matter.

While talking with an engineer, he relayed that his most difficult college project was to create an inverted pendulum. Finding that perfect balance was, as he shared, nearly impossible.

In order for a pendulum to stand up straight it must be perfectly balanced, experiencing the same amount of pull from each side. It is only the equal distribution of tension which allows the pendulum to remain upright. With even the slightest variation in pressure from one side or the other, the pendulum will fall.

I believe this also speaks well to the necessary balance of the Christian life. Having an equal appreciation for the law and freedom is essential to a healthy outlook. Without balance, the options are varying degrees of decadence or piety. The same could be said of almost any area of our life. Too much drive can lead to obsession, not enough can lead to starvation. And the pendulum hanging in the middle is simply a lifeless thing which has succumbed to the earth's gravitational pull.

....

Discuss: *Psalm 25:20–22* and *Galatians 5:13*
Are there areas of your life needing to be brought into balance?
For additional discussion read *Romans 8:20–22* and *Ephesians 6:12*.
Talk about the balance between these two texts.

What will consume you?

*… let us be thankful, and so worship God acceptably
with reverence and awe, for our "God is a consuming fire."*

—Hebrews 12:28–29 NIV

BELIEVE IT WAS SAINT AUGUSTINE who first spoke of the God-shaped void which exists within each of us. It is the aching created by this unfilled void, which I believe drives us to chase false gods and feed addictions.

A few years ago, I heard the story of an Egyptian billionaire who was sentenced to be hanged for his involvement in the murder of a young woman. I remember thinking how sad it was that this man's desire for revenge would so consume him he would take the risk of forfeiting not just his fortune, but his life.

As I considered this, I began to think about all the things with which mankind can so easily be consumed: anger, bitterness, jealousy, substance, career, even religion can distract us from the joy and peace of God's love and the purpose it affords.

It was this thought which inspired our song "Consume Me,"[12] and the words of the second verse speak directly to it. "I've traveled down so many roads and seen many things, and all have left me wanting for more. But now, here in Your presence, I have everything I need. You're all my heart was longing for."

We all have things which can consume us. Not all of them in and of themselves are sinful, but if allowed to have a higher priority in our lives than our relationship with God they are altogether wrong.

Discuss:

What areas of your life are prone to consume you?

How are we best able to see them clearly and prioritize them properly?

39

Good science

....

> *For in Him all things were created: things*
> *in Heaven and on earth, visible and invisible.*
> *—Colossians 1:16 NIV*

RECENTLY SAW A BUMPER STICKER which read: "Science: Man trying to figure out what God has done." That simple, yet profound statement provided me with a great deal of mental fodder as I considered the wonders of creation.

There are many areas in life we are tempted to compartmentalize: this is my work life, this is my social life, this is my church life, and so forth. But, there are no two areas more prone to be viewed through completely different lenses, in my opinion, than faith and science.

As Christians, I believe compartmentalization to be both naive and dangerous. Our goal should be consistency, and while we do interact differently with an old friend than we do a business colleague, we should always strive to be us.

I believe the same consistency should be present in our thoughts concerning faith and science, and it is the bumper sticker's message which answers the obvious why. When we are researching everything from the deepest galaxies of space, to the amazing complexities of DNA, the *simple cell*—which is anything but simple—the earth's gravitational pull, or anything else for that matter, the realization that it was created by God gives us reason to be both awed and simultaneously affirmed in our faith.

Science is not something we have to make fit into our Christian faith. When we have the courage to view it objectively it will always fit, hand in glove.

....

Read and discuss: *Psalm 139:13–16* and *Genesis 1:14–19*
What do these verses say about how things came into being?
Why do you think faith is often dismissed from scientific studies?

Scars and other beautiful things

....

... by His wounds we are healed.

—Isaiah 53:5 NIV

S CARS ARE VERY OBVIOUS REMINDERS of past hurts; maybe it was an accident, surgery, or abuse, which caused our body to be scarred, but long after our physical healing, emotional wounds can remain, continuing to fester deep beneath the surface, poisoning our spirit and isolating our soul.

We are often prone to cover our scars with clothing, make up, or even plastic surgery because we consider them unsightly or embarrassing, but they actually hold within them a certain beauty. While scars are a constant reminder of our pain, they are also evidence of God's healing mercy. Therefore, bearing our scars openly provides us a platform on which we can freely share His redemptive work in our lives.

The dictionary defines redemption this way: "to buy or pay off; clear by payment, to recover, to convert, to make up for, to obtain the release or restoration of, as by paying a ransom." As Christians, we understand it is through Christ's suffering and death we receive the opportunity of redemption.

When we are willing to share the stories surrounding our scars in an effort to help others, we are, in effect, redeeming our pain for a greater purpose: love. Love provides the ransom demanded by bitter memories, releases us from anger and fear, and once again allows us to freely enjoy the peace of God's affection, long since denied us by our wounded heart.

....

Read: *Isaiah 35* **(Joy of the Redeemed)**

Talk about the hope reflected in this passage. Can you think of anyone who, because of their willingness to share their scars, has encouraged you?

Are you willing to uncover your scars, when need be, to help others?

If it is possible

....

If it is possible, as far as it depends on you,
live at peace with everyone.

—*Romans 12:18 NIV*

UNLESS YOU LIVE UNDER A ROCK, you likely have at least one and possibly a few people in your life with whom it is almost impossible to get along.

As Christians, we should desire to live at peace with everyone, being willing to die to ourselves, turn the other cheek, and go the extra mile as the Bible encourages. But, when dealing with difficult people, sometimes the more we seemingly give, the more we are expected to take. For years, I lived life believing in order to be a good Christian and live at peace with others, I had to be a doormat, but I found release from this false assumption in Romans 12:18.

While we are not called to be doormats, we also are not called to be spiritual bullies. I particularly appreciate the way the apostle Peter encourages us to live out our faith: "… in your hearts revere Christ as Lord. Always be prepared to give an answer to everyone who asks you to give the reason for the hope that you have. But do this with gentleness and respect …" (1 Peter 3:15)

Living at peace with others can present its challenges and require serious gut checks, but sometimes the only peace we are able to find comes from within. A dear friend and mentor taught me to *pick my battles*. Doing so requires thought and self examination prior to engagement. When we consider the long term implications of our actions we are much more likely to be led by the Spirit and less by our flesh, which will afford us peace, even when chaos surrounds us.

....

Discuss: *1 Peter 3:15* and *Romans 12:18*
How might these verses help us view difficult personalities with a proper perspective?

2+2=5?

....

If you hold to My teaching, you are really My disciples.
Then you will know the truth and the truth will set you free.
—John 8:31–32 NIV

IN OUR CONTEMPORARY, politically correct society, we often hear things like "truth is relative" and "we can decide our own truth." That philosophy may get you points for tolerance, but at the end of the day, it does not make you right. You can convince yourself there is no such thing as gravity, but if you jump off a building you are not going to float. You can truly believe 2+2=5, but if that is your answer on a test you will get it wrong every time. Truth is still truth whether we choose to believe it or not.

But what is truth and how do we find it? I believe it starts with a humble heart willing to take every thought and word captive, willing to ask the tough questions and admit when we do not have the answers, and being willing to deny ourselves allowing our agendas to take a back seat to the truth as it is made evident. I believe when we do this, we will find the truth. And what is that truth? It is a person and His name is Jesus.

1 Timothy 2:3–5 says it this way: "This is good and acceptable in the sight of God our Savior, who desires all men to be saved and to come to the knowledge of the truth. For there is one God, and one mediator also between God and men, the man Christ Jesus …".

....

Read and discuss: *John 14:6* and *2 Thessalonians 2:9–11*

Trusting God
in difficult times

....

I consider that our present sufferings
are not worth comparing with the glory
that will be revealed in us.

—Romans 8:18 NIV

Hope knows that if great trials are avoided,
great deeds remain undone, and the possibility of growth
into greatness of soul is aborted.

—Brennan Manning,
Abba's Child[13]

Remember what Bilbo used to say:
It's a dangerous business, Frodo, going out your door.
You step onto the road, and if you don't keep your feet,
there's no knowing where you might be swept off to.

—J.R.R. Tolkien,
The Lord of the Rings:
The Fellowship of the Ring[14]

Where is God?

....

*'Truly, I say to you, as you did it to one of the least of these
my brothers, you did it to me."*
—Matthew 25:40 NLT

S O OFTEN, WHEN IN A TRAUMATIC SITUATION, whether disease, accident, or natural disaster, we hear people ask: "Where is God?"

Over the last few years our nation has been rocked by hurricanes, tornados, floods, droughts, wildfires, and the like. Stories of mass murders are not uncommon, and my children can barely remember a time when we were not at war.

Yet in spite of pain and adversity, God is with us. It is easy to wonder why God allows bad things to happen. But the fact is, we live in a fallen world. God created and called it good; then, sin entered the world and with it came the chaos we now know as normal.

Our song, "Where is God"[15] was inspired as we watched the news reports from the 2010 Haitian earthquake. We saw not only pictures of devastation, but glimpses of hope afforded to those in need through the work of the many volunteers who poured into the island nation in the days and weeks following the earthquake.

Jesus said in Matthew 18:20 that when two or three come together in His name, He is with them. When we serve those in need—"the least of these"—we serve Christ, as referenced above. At the same time we, as the Body of Christ, are His hands and feet. It is this amazing truth we were considering as we put the finishing touches on the lyrics of "Where is God?" "Locked in a prison of my sickness, you took my hand, felt the love of Jesus when you called me friend."

....

Discuss:

Have you ever served someone in need?

Have you ever been served in a time of need?

How did this make you feel?

What are some needs you see today?

How might you help?

God's perfect plan

Kaylyn Frye

....

> *"For I know the plans that I have for you," declares the LORD,*
> *"plans for welfare and not for calamity to give you a future*
> *and a hope."*
>
> —*Jeremiah 29:11 NASB*

IT IS VERY NORMAL TO DREAM, to imagine where life will take us and how we might get there. Often, we think we know exactly how our desires will play out—then, in an instant, we are faced with the unexpected—the proverbial game changer, and suddenly our dreams appear out of reach.

On September 28, 2009, my family and I were traveling home from a weekend of concerts when we received a call informing us that one of our dearest friends had been in an accident which had left him paralyzed below the sternum.

He had just begun his senior year in high school and was looking forward to perusing a career as a pilot after graduation, but as the reality of his new normal set in, his dream of flying seemed all but impossible. However, as we are reminded in Luke 1:37, "… nothing is impossible with God."

Because of the paralysis, doors opened which otherwise would not have been available, and in the spring of 2012 he moved to Colorado to begin training as a helicopter pilot.

The road which leads to our dreams is often more difficult than we expect, complete with detours and roadblocks. It can try our patience and test our resolve, but it is often because of these very challenges we have the strength and skills to realize our dreams.

....

Discuss: *Proverbs 16:3*
What does it mean to commit our plans to the Lord?
Are you willing to battle life's unexpected challenges to accomplish your dreams?

God of the last resort

....

But seek first His kingdom and His righteousness,
and all these things will be given to you as well.
—*Matthew 6:33 NIV*

HOW MANY TIMES HAVE WE TRIED to figure things out on our own, solve our own problems, and map out our own destiny instead of simply seeking God's leading right from the start? I am learning that when I am willing to take God at His word and seek Him first, I not only spare myself a lot of headaches and anxiety but save valuable time in the process.

Sometimes our detours into self-reliance last only a few days, other times we can stubbornly hold onto our hurts, fears, and agendas for years, even taking them to our graves, never fully surrendering our right to blaze our own trail or hide in our self-imposed prison. In doing so, we deny ourselves the fullness of the peace which is only found in the center of God's will.

Maybe we consider our problems too trivial to bother the Creator of the Universe, or possibly, we feel such oppressing shame we cannot bring ourselves to utter even a simple prayer. No matter our situation, God cares. The small stuff is not small to God; if it concerns us, no matter the size, it concerns Him.

Do you know how much you occupy the thoughts of God? Psalm 139:17–18 tells us, "How precious to me are Your thoughts, O God How vast is the sum of them! Were I to count them, they would outnumber the grains of sand..." We so consume the thoughts of God that He not only knows the number of hairs on our head (Matthew 10:30), but Isaiah tells us He has engraved us on the palms of His hands. (Isaiah 49:16) Amazing!

....

Consider:

Are there times you are tempted to rely on your own reason rather than trusting fully in the loving sovereignty of God?

Is God typically your first response or your last resort?

Living in the fall

....

… My grace is sufficient for you …

—2 Corinthians 12:9 NIV

IT IS **8:48** ON EASTER MORNING, Resurrection Sunday. My family is at church, while I am home, sick. It is not just a normal bug, but a condition which flairs up occasionally and when it does, I am down for a few days. All things considered, I have nothing to complain about. I know people, good people, who love the Lord, and have for years struggled with maladies far worse than mine.

In times such as these, I am reminded of two things: the effects of the fall and the promise of our Redeemer—the first born of the grave—whose resurrection we celebrate today.

In our culture, the "name it and claim it" message has become quite popular. It says if we have enough faith to claim healing as truth, we will indeed be healed. Though understandably popular, I believe it to be a dangerous message. It is easy to pull a verse from here and there and claim it as truth, but when seeking answers to life's questions we need to consider the whole of Scripture. Don't get me wrong, I know God heals. I have seen it first hand, but sometimes He also allows suffering to persist.

When we accept the "name it and claim it" ideology as truth, and thereby hold to the belief that we can somehow demand healing of God, we set ourselves up to potentially question His goodness, if not His very existence. In doing so, we can give fear a foothold by falsely assuming our faith is somehow anemic.

Paul speaks of a "thorn in his flesh" which he pleaded for God to remove. God's response: "My grace is sufficient for you, for My power is made perfect in weakness." While this message may not be the most popular, it is truth nonetheless.

....

Read and discuss: *2 Corinthians 12:1–10*
What thorns might you have?
What do you think God's response meant to Paul?
What do you think God's response means for you?

The blessed

....

... blessed is the man who trusts in the Lord,
  whose confidence is in Him.

—*Jeremiah 17:7 NIV*

HAVE YOU EVER NOTICED a tree which, though appearing healthy, had fallen as a result of a storm or worse yet, succumbed merely to its own weight? A closer look often reveals a rotten core or maybe a poor root system.

Shallow roots can be the result of poor soil conditions, such as those referenced in *The Parable of the Sower* (Matthew 13:21) or even from a lack of resistance or stress.

In the early 1990s, a group of scientist took part in an experiment called *Biosphere 2*, which required them to live in a seemingly perfect environment for two years. Interestingly though, during the course of their experiment, trees inside the dome began to topple beneath their own weight. It was determined this was caused by the lack of *reaction wood* or *stress wood* as it is also known. Stress wood develops as a result of resistance, including wind, found in the less than perfect conditions of the real world.

There are times in our lives when we face resistance as well. Emotional storms and drought can threaten our very existence, but as the Prophet Jeremiah reminds us, when our trust is in the Lord, there is no need to fear. Though less than ideal conditions exist around us, we can continue to bear fruit because our hope is rooted not in our circumstance but in God alone.

....

Consider and discuss:

How do you respond to adversity?

With hope?

With fear?

Looking back, what difficulties have you faced which have ultimately strengthened your faith?

Read: *Jeremiah 17:5–8*

Compare and contrast what the prophet tells us about trusting in man, verses trusting in God.

It is seldom what you think

… weakness was turned to strength …

—Hebrews 11:34 NIV

I NEVER WANTED TO BE A MUSICIAN. Though it looked fun, I knew I did not have what it takes and, even if I did, the thought of standing in front of an audience was quite intimidating … no, it was down right paralyzing.

I never wanted to be in ministry, either. It looked anything but fun; in fact, I thought it seemed stuffy, boring, and more of a cause for uptightness than freedom. But here I am in music ministry and loving it! God truly has a sense of humor.

I first began to feel a passion for ministry one Sunday while listening to a sermon by a guest speaker. In his words, I heard not only boldness and authority but passion, and for the first time in my life I thought, *If this is ministry, count me in!*

At the same time, people began to affirm my songwriting ability, suggesting I "do something" with it. My response was always the same: "I don't do that." It took a few years for me to realize my music was my ministry, and so, reluctantly, I began to "do that."

If there is one thing I have learned over the years, it is this: If you surrender to God, He will certainly use you, but seldom as you might expect. I have told the musicians I mentor many times, "Always live expecting God to be at work in your life, but never live in such a way as to place expectations upon Him."

I believe most often God uses us specifically in areas where we are not comfortable, simply to keep us dependant on Him. This dependence results in trust and in trust we receive the boldness and strength needed to achieve our purpose.

Read and discuss: *Hebrews 11*
Ask yourself where you feel most vulnerable.
Are you willing to use that very part of your life to point others to Christ?

Traveling through the wilderness

He changes a wilderness into a pool of water
and a dry land into springs of water.
—Psalm 107:35 NASB

I AM A NERD WHEN IT COMES TO album liner notes. I enjoy reading the lyrics, who wrote the songs, played the instruments, produced the album, the whole nine yards. Not only do I enjoy liner notes, but I also find the artwork and album titles equally as interesting. So, as you can imagine, though it may not matter nearly as much to anyone else, I spend a lot of time on liner notes.

As we were recording the *Songs of a Wilderness Traveler* album, I was struggling to come up with a title which captured the essence of the project, so a friend volunteered to help. I sent her some early mixes of the songs and as she listened, she concluded most of the songs sounded as if I had written them while in a spiritual wilderness. She was right.

Most were indeed inspired as I wandered through a difficult season, during which much of what had been familiar or comfortable had either vanished or had been revealed as nothing more than a mirage of hope and security. As I thought back to that time, I recalled many heroes of our faith who had also spent time in the wilderness: Moses, David, Elijah, Paul, and of course Jesus being numbered among them. This helped me understand the necessity of the wilderness both in the revelation and affirmation of our call and for the solidification of our resolve. It is in the wilderness, when all is stripped away, we truly realize our utter dependence on Jehovah Jireh—*The Lord Who Provides*.

It is only natural to avoid the wilderness. Maybe it is because we cling too tightly to our titles, relationships, or creature comforts. But it is only in the wilderness we learn the true meaning of trust.

Read: *Luke 12:22–34*
Talk about God's provision in your life.

Weeds

....

And the one on whom seed was sown on the good soil,
this is the man who hears the word and understands it;
who indeed bears fruit and brings forth, some a hundredfold,
some sixty, and some thirty.

—Matthew 13:23 NASB

I LOVE TO GARDEN. The smell of the dirt as it is tilled in the spring, the first sight of green shoots poking through the ground, and the taste of freshly picked sweet corn; the whole process is something I truly enjoy.

A garden does require regular, almost daily, attention. Between the tilling of the soil and the harvesting of the crop, there is the planting, watering, pruning, keeping an eye out for those plant eating pests, and then there are the weeds.

It takes great effort to grow a crop, but weeds just happen. They are the first to sprout and the last to die, they need no nurturing to flourish and are quite able to exist in the worst of conditions (I once even saw a weed growing from a crack in a brick). These energy robbing products of the curse serve only to siphon off valuable nutrients, weakening the plant and lowering the yield.

It is the same way in life. Discipleship takes deliberate effort, constant awareness and time, but bad habits and attitudes can creep up before we know it, choking the joy right out of us, and distracting our attention from our fruit-bearing purpose.

Then comes the harvest when we are rewarded for our diligence with delicious, life giving fruit. But, no matter how tasty, I am confident the best ear of sweet corn is but a dim foretaste of the wonderful bounty we will enjoy at the banquet table, as we partake in the wedding feast of the Lamb.

....

Read and discuss: *Matthew 13:1–43*

The path of least resistance

....

> *Enter through the narrow gate. For wide is the gate and broad
> is the road that leads to destruction, and many enter through it.
> But small is the gate and narrow the road that leads to life, and
> only a few find it.*
>
> —*Matthew 7:13–14 NIV*

THE AVERAGE ADULT BODY is made up of more than sixty percent water, and water as you know, unless forced to do otherwise, always follows the path of least resistance. So it stands to reason as humans we are often tempted to *go with the flow*. Though the easy life, as it were, may be leisurely for a season, in the long run it leads to complacency and then to stagnation.

In Mitch McVicker's[16] song "Upside Down" he sings, "I'm living in a world that's upside down … but someday I'll see God." When following Christ, it seems we often find ourselves feeling as though we are "upside down," as we fight the societal currents and buck contemporary trends.

During those difficult times it can seem as though things would be easier if we just gave into the pressures and coasted through life. In these moments we must be willing to echo the words of Zechariah's song, "… in the shadow of death, … guide our feet into the path of peace" (Luke 1:79). As we are reminded in Matthew 7:13–14, it is the broad road—the path of least resistance—which leads to destruction, and the narrow road which leads to life!

....

Discuss:

In what ways might you be tempted to follow the path of least resistance?

Talk about the possible implications of the *life* as referenced in *Matthew 7:13–14*.

Total commitment

*… in all things God works for the good of those who love Him,
who have been called according to His purpose.*

—*Romans 8:28 NIV*

T HE ISRAELITES WERE TRAPPED. In front of them lay the Red Sea, behind them Pharaoh's mighty army. The situation appeared bleak, to say the least. Then God did what He always does for those who follow Him—He made a way. Moses raised his staff and stretched his hand over the waters just as God had instructed. The sea parted, and the Israelites walked across to safety.

Years later, as the children of Israel were about to enter the Promised Land, they were stopped, once again, by a body of water. This time it was the flooded Jordan River. They could see their new home on the other side, but the flood waters kept them from entering. God again demonstrated His might by parting the waters, but this time, instead of outstretched hands, He required a full-fledged step of faith. The Priests carrying the Ark of the Covenant were instructed to walk into the river. Picture this: as the Levites carrying the Ark reached the river's edge, they raised their feet, shifted their weight, and stepped, and the river parted, but not until their feet touched the water (Joshua 3:15–16)! That is faith! That is commitment! That is total trust!

Often times in our faith walk, God requires the same of us. We all would rather have Him part the waters ahead of us, but sometimes He requires us to trust Him enough to put everything on the line. This can be downright unnerving, but God does not call us to a life of safety and security; He calls us to follow Him. And as it was with the Levites, it is with us: When we put our faith in God, He always shows up, right on time!

Discuss:
Share about a time when God made a way for you.

Peace

....

The steadfast of mind You will keep in perfect peace,
because He trusts in You. Trust in the LORD forever …
—Isaiah 26:3–4 NASB

PRE-CONCERT JITTERS ARE NORMAL, but today was different; today I felt particularly anxious. There was a time when just the thought of being in front of a crowd would have made me want to turn and run in the opposite direction, giving into my fears and forsaking my call. Were it not for the confidence of knowing it was God opening the door into music ministry, I would have never made it past my first stage appearance. This has taught me a valuable life lesson: Meeting our fears head on is an essential requirement to overcoming them.

Today, however, I was singing at a funeral, and though an honor, times such as these always bring their share of stressors. As I walked into the church's backroom to collect my thoughts and clear my mind, I noticed a framed Bible verse hanging on the wall: Isaiah 26:3. I do not know how long it had been there, but I felt as though it was hung there just for me, just for this moment. I took a deep breath, thanked God for His perfect peace, and went into the sanctuary to await the beginning of the service.

Life presents its share of difficult situations. While in the midst of them, it is essential that we fix our hearts and minds on the perfect peace of our Lord. Focusing on anything else serves only to feed our fears and distract our focus, limiting our ability to give our full and undivided attention to that which we are called.

....

Consider:

Do you have a heart to serve and yet are prone to yield to anxiety or fear?

How might considering today's verse help you move forward in the calm assurance of your call?

Adversity

....

I have told you these things, so that you may have peace.
In this world you will have trouble. But take heart!
I have overcome the world.

—*John 16:33 NIV*

HAVE YOU EVER HEARD THE PHRASE, "What doesn't kill you makes you stronger"? Adversity does unequivocally bring out either the best or the worst in people. While some succumb immediately, bending beneath the weight of the circumstance, others attempt to ignore any sense of conflict avoiding as long as possible all associated discomfort, and a few dare to stand and valiantly face their foe with inspirational courage and defiant peace.

Trouble can come in any number of ways: through natural disaster or disease, intentional or accidental consequences of our own actions or those of others, or even by willful destruction, but it is those who courageously look beyond the temporal who truly understand the peace and hope of Christ.

When facing adversity, I am reminded of two songs. A children's song based on the parable of *The Wise and Foolish Builders* found in Matthew 7:24–27, which says in part, "The wise man built his house upon the rock," and the song "Bound to Come Some Trouble" by Rich Mullins,[17] which opens with these lyrics, "There's bound to come some trouble to your life, but that ain't nothing to be afraid of. There's bound to come some trouble to your life, but that ain't no reason to fear. I know there's bound to come some trouble to your life, but reach out to Jesus and hold on tight. He's been there before and He knows what it's like. You'll find He's there."

Trouble is not optional; where we choose to build is.

....

Read: *Matthew 7:24–27*
Talk about the importance of having a foundation of faith.

God thoughts

....

> *How precious to me are Your thoughts, O God!*
> *How vast is the sum of them!*
> —*Psalm 139:17 NIV*

HAVE YOU EVER HEARD SOMETHING over and over again? I am not talking about the hottest new radio single that seems to get played every 20 minutes. I mean a thought, a phrase or Bible verse? My wife Lisa and I call those *God thoughts* or *God winks*.

In 2002 I lost one of my dearest boyhood friends. His death was quite unexpected. Will was one of those friends who knew everything about you and loved you anyway, and his passing left a big hole in many lives.

In the days following his death I remember praying, "God, I know You have a plan and I don't have to like it, but can You at least help me make some sense of this?"

Over the next few weeks I began to hear Psalm 139 repeatedly: in a conversation with a friend, Lisa referencing it during school as I walked through the room, and from the pastor in a random episode of *Little House on the Prairie*. God seemed to be doing everything but read it to me audibly, and then … He did!

I was listening to Chuck Swindoll's[18] radio program as I pulled into a parking lot, and I heard him say to the congregation, "I want you to close your eyes as I read for you this passage." I thought, *OK Chuck, I'll bite and sit here for a few more minutes*. He proceeded to read the entire 139th Psalm, and I wept, realizing not only how I had been missing His clues, but also how much His love and patience far exceeded my lack of perception. God is good and His thoughts are indeed precious!

....

Discuss: Take a few moments to read *Psalm 139*.

What does this passage say about God's involvement in your life?

Have you ever experienced a God *wink*?

How did it make you feel?

Lay it down

....

*... because you have done this and have not withheld your son,
your only son, I will surely bless you ...*

—Genesis 22:16–17 NIV

THERE ARE FEW STORIES which epitomize faith more vividly than that of Abraham's near sacrifice of his son, Isaac. God promised Abraham and Sarah a son. They waited and waited. Then came the joy of the promise fulfilled, followed a few years later by God making an unthinkable request of Abraham: to offer his promised son as a sacrifice.

God certainly knows our heart better than we do. I believe it is for this reason He sometimes requires of us extraordinary sacrifice. Not because He wants to rob our joy, but in order that we might truly know *our* own hearts, understanding fully the lengths to which we are willing to go to be obedient, assuring ourselves of God's true place in our lives.

When we are willing to lay our hopes, dreams, and desires upon the altar of sacrifice, we are truly saying *God, I love you more*. This not only reveals the depth of our love, but like Abraham, it affirms our faith in God. Abraham demonstrated his incredible faith as he and Isaac began their climb up the mountain. Having everything needed for the sacrifice, except the sacrifice itself, Abraham told his servant, "We will worship and then we will come back to you" (Genesis 22:5).

I do not believe Abraham knew *how* God was going to do it, but he knew God's promises were trustworthy, and for this reason, he could be certain he and his son would return. This story has reminded me many times of God's faithfulness, and has helped me to see the necessity of trusting God in all things.

....

Read and discuss: *Genesis 22:1–19*
Are there things in your life you find difficult to part with?
How might this story help?

How much can I get away with?

....

... all our righteous acts are like filthy rags ...
—Isaiah 64:6 NIV

ONE OF THE MANY FADS OF THE 80s was buttons. Buttons pinned on jackets and book bags, carrying any number of messages— from our favorite pop stars, to sarcastic comments, and a few that actually shared positive messages. Being a teen in the 80s I had my share of buttons. I remember one which read, "How much can I get away with and still go to Heaven?" At the time I found it amusing, but looking back, I see it was actually a testament to my lack of truly understanding the meaning of goodness.

When I was growing up, I was taught that our biggest goals as Christians were to be good and go to Heaven. Certainly both are fine ideas, but following Jesus is much more than a list of *dos and don'ts*, and our hope should not only be to someday go to Heaven but also to desire the Kingdom that is available to us now. After all, goodness does not guarantee a place in Heaven. Not only that, but I have found goodness can be quite a distraction to the very faith I profess.

If our goal is nothing more than goodness and serving a list of rules and regulations our only standard, we can become so secure in our self-righteousness we risk making an idol of our piety, all the while neglecting the very God we claim to serve. This wrong focus will likely lead to frustration instead of freedom, and ultimately bring us to pose questions like the one on my button. We are not, after all, saved by our goodness but by the goodness of Christ, and once He becomes our main focus, everything else will fall into place.

....

Discuss: Have you grown weary of trying to be good?
Read *Mark 10:18* and *John 15:1–17*.
What do these verses have to say about goodness?
What are the keys to bearing good fruit?

Broken

....

Submit yourselves, then, to God.
Resist the devil, and he will flee from you.

—*James 4:7 NIV*

ONE OF THE MOST SATISFYING EXPERIENCES I have ever had was breaking my horse, Junior. It was, in spite of what most people would imagine, a relatively simple and gratifying process, the greatest requirement being time from the very beginning: touching, loving, and earning his trust. The Native Americans called this imprinting. While there were moments of correction, most of the time was simply spent handling him—the first time I was ever on his back I rode him seven miles without incident.

"Breaking a horse" is not really about "breaking" them; it is more about teaching them to use their strength for good. If you truly have to "break" a horse, it is difficult and sometimes impossible and is usually the result of not having the "imprinting" experience.

When a horse is unbroken he is a danger not only to himself but also to those around him. The same is true of us. After all, brokenness is simply about submission. When we understand this truth we are then able to trust the hands which not only formed us in our mother's womb but also direct our steps. Only then are we able to use our energy to its fullest potential, saving ourselves a lot of grief and frustration along the way.

....

Read and discuss: *James 4:1–12*
What do these verses say about submission?

Are there any areas of your life that you have struggled to submit (trust) to God?

The resurrection and the life

....

"I am the resurrection and the life.
The one who believes in Me will live, even though they die ..."
—*John 11:25 NIV*

THIS WEEK, TWO SOMBER OCCASIONS were very much at the forefront of my mind. Locally, our community was mourning the loss of a soldier killed in Afghanistan, and personally, I was remembering one of my dearest friends on the tenth anniversary of his passing.

With these two men so predominately in my thoughts, it is no wonder one morning this week I woke from a dream about each of their funerals. As I lie in my bed, my mind racing with the details of the dream, Jesus' words "I am the Resurrection and the Life" echoed in my mind. The reality of the resurrected Christ, the First Born of the grave, and the Hope of life eternal, provided me with a sense of peace and comfort which does not typically follow such a dream.

I recall attending a church service where someone once asked for prayer for the family of one whose "body had died." What a great perspective. This simple yet profound truth has comforted me on many occasions since and has served as a powerful reminder that my hope lies solely in Jesus.

While death is inevitable, we can rest in the assurance that "to live is Christ and to die is gain" (Philippians 1:21). Though none of us look forward to pain and loss, as followers of Jesus, it is this truth which sustains us during the most difficult of times, allowing us to "mourn, but not as those without hope" (1 Thessalonians 4:14). A hope which bears witness to the Gospel even during our most difficult moments.

....

Read: *1 Thessalonians 4:13–18*

How are these verses and those referenced above an "encouragement" during our times of loss?

Mountains

....

I will lift up my eyes to the mountains;
from where shall my help come?
My help comes from the LORD, Who made heaven and earth.
He will not allow your foot to slip;
He who keeps you will not slumber.

—Psalm 121:1–3 NAS

As I write this, I am sitting in a hotel room in Colorado Springs. The sun is setting over the mountains, perfectly silhouetting Pike's Peak. In this majestic moment, I am reminded of the promise held in the Psalm referenced above.

Mountains are often used as a metaphor when describing difficult circumstances. Like the mountains, our troubles can often appear insurmountable. Disheartened, we can easily succumb to our fears, sinking ever deeper into the valley of the shadow. But, as the Psalmist also clearly reminds us in Psalm 139:7–10, God is always with us: "Where can I go from Your Spirit? Where can I flee from Your presence? If I go up to the heavens, You are there. If I make my bed in the depths You are there. If I rise on the wings of the dawn, if I settle on the far side of the sea, even there Your hand will guide me, Your right hand will hold me fast."

It is in the assurance of God's presence we find the strength to lift our eyes to the mountains and face our adversary. Trusting in His guidance, we find the confidence needed to begin the long journey up the mountain.

....

Discuss:

What mountains are you facing?

How does the knowledge of God's presence make facing your mountains easier?

How have you experienced God's hand guiding you or His right hand holding you fast as referenced in *Psalm 139:10*?

Abiding

Just as the Father has loved Me, I have also loved you; abide in My love. If you keep My commandments, you will abide in My love; just as I have kept My Father's commandments and abide in His love. These things I have spoken to you so that My joy may be in you, and that your joy may be made full. "This is My commandment, that you love one another, just as I have loved you. Greater love has no one than this, that one lay down his life for his friends. You are My friends if you do what I command you. No longer do I call you slaves, for the slave does not know what his master is doing; but I have called you friends, for all things that I have heard from My Father I have made known to you.

—John 15:9–15 NASB

Even though I walk through the valley of the shadow of death, I fear no evil, for You are with me; Your rod and Your staff, they comfort me. You prepare a table before me in the presence of my enemies; You have anointed my head with oil; My cup overflows. Surely goodness and lovingkindness will follow me all the days of my life, And I will dwell in the house of the LORD forever.

—Psalm 23:4–6 NASB

"Ah, there is rest!" I thought. "I have striven in vain to rest in Him. I'll strive no more. For has He not promised to abide with me— never to leave me, never to fail me?"

—Hudson Taylor
19th Century Missionary to China[19]

Faith without works

....

... faith without deeds is useless.

—James 2:20 NIV

NCLUDED IN MY RATHER LONG LIST of favorite Rich Mullins songs is "Screen Door," which takes a lighthearted look at the relationship between faith and works. "Faith without works, it's like a song you can't sing. It's about as useless as a screen door on a submarine."[20]

Recently I had a conversation with a friend who confessed to me his own struggle to reconcile the relationship between works (or goodness) and faith. He related that for years he dizzied himself with the knowledge that while we are not saved by our goodness, as Christians, we are often prone to act as though our salvation is utterly dependent upon how well we keep the rules.

For years, I struggled with the same thing, but it was the simple phrase, *We are not saved because we're good, we're good because we're saved*, which finally helped me come to terms with the role goodness plays in the life of the believer.

Goodness is neither a down payment nor a retainer for our salvation. In fact, our goodness alone has no bearing on our eternal destiny. Goodness is simply a natural response of the life lived in the light of God's love.

Jesus said in Luke 6:43–44, "No good tree bears bad fruit, nor does a bad tree bear good fruit. Each tree is recognized by its own fruit."

In the end, true goodness is nothing we are capable of producing. It is simply the result of abiding in God (John 15:1–17). Therefore it is not the means by which we earn God's favor, but rather the evidence of His goodness flowing through us.

....

Read: *Luke 6:43–45* and *James 2:14–26*
Are you keenly aware of God's blessings in your life?
How are you responding to them?

Boundaries

....

May Your compassion come to me that I may live,
For Your law is my delight.

—*Psalm 119:77 NASB*

BOUNDARIES ARE SOMETHING WE ALL CRAVE. They may not sound like anything we want or need, but we do and they are. When raised without boundaries, a child will often respond by withdrawing or acting out, searching for those illusive and sometimes mobile markers which need to be established by their parents in order that the child might know a sense of stability.

I am reminded of one particular episode of the old television series *Family Affair*.[21] In it, Buffy and Jodi, twins being raised by their uncle, decided they were tired of rules and lobbied their uncle to live free of restraint. Seeing an opportunity for a valuable life lesson, their uncle relented, allowing the siblings to decide what they ate, when they went to bed, etc. It took only a few days for their poor diet and inconsistent sleep habits to catch up with them, and they soon found themselves wanting for the security of their uncle's boundaries.

I have seen this in my own life as well. My parents shared little, if any, of the same values, so my boundaries varied tremendously depending on whether I was with either or both of them, their moods at the moment, and any number of other outside influences. This lack of clearly established boundaries caused me to retreat and contributed greatly to my sense of fear and insecurity. Consequently, as an adult, I have had to labor through the cause and effect of instability, painstakingly seeking to establish healthy boundaries. And though nagging doubts sometimes persist, God's grace and patience continues to provide an ever increasing flow of peace.

....

Read and discuss: *Psalm 119:173–175*

The record deal

....

*Trust in the Lord with all your heart and lean not on your own
understanding; in all your ways acknowledge Him and He will
make your path straight.*

—Proverbs 3:5–6 NIV

I ONCE HEARD A CHRISTIAN RECORDING ARTIST say during a concert, "God
is a lot like our earthly father. If we want something, we just need to
crawl up in His lap and bat our eyes and He will give it to us." I almost
fell out of the pew. Then, this artist went on to say they wanted a
record deal so bad they presented God with this ultimatum: "Give me
a deal or take my voice." I remember thinking, *If I prayed that, I would
surely come down with a case of permanent laryngitis*. The story
continued, complete with a record deal, and I found myself perplexed.

Six months later I learned the label went bankrupt and all their
recordings were tied up in litigation. I am not sure what to make of
this, except to say I think it is OK to ask God for anything. Throughout
Scripture we are repeatedly told to ask, but if we are to follow Christ's
example, we also need to include, "Not my will but Yours be done."

We often confuse our *wants* and *needs* and certainly are prone to
look to others for validation. Without a record deal, we may question
our legitimacy as an artist, or if our kids do not wear the latest fashions
we might feel as though we are an inadequate provider. But the fact
of the matter is, in submitting ourselves to this kind of pressure we
are looking to others, not to God, for affirmation and through our
actions confessing our willingness to follow our desires rather than
God's direction.

....

Discuss:

Are there areas of your life in which you struggle to trust God?

Why do you think trust is such a difficult thing?

What do you think it means to acknowledge God in all our ways?

Living our dream

Lisa Frye

....

> *For we are co-workers in God's service;*
> *you are God's field, God's building.*
>
> **—1 Corinthians 3:9 NIV**

WE ALL HAVE DREAMS. Some are rooted in our God-given passions, while others have more to do with our own desires. While our wants are not always bad, the key to living out our dream (purpose) begins with the ability to recognize the difference.

We live in a nearly 100 year old house in a small, Indiana town, which would be more accurately described as a rural neighborhood. When we moved here as a young couple we had no intention of making this our home. However, as the children came along, followed by our decision that I would be a stay-at-home mom and later to homeschool, it became obvious that while our house was not the home of our dreams, it made it possible for us to continue to raise our family as we wanted.

Though I am thankful for our home, not having all the amenities my dream-house would offer can sometimes take my attitude on a bit of a detour. That is when I have to remind myself of my true passion and purpose: being a wife and mother.

One day, as our family was visiting a local nursing home, one of the residents asked where we lived. She was pleased to find out we lived in her home-town and asked which house was ours. When we told her, she replied, "That was always my dream house." This was a bit of a reality check for me as I realized I was living someone else's dream. It was also a good reminder that when we are focused only on our wants it is hard to feel content no matter where we are. While our wants may provide momentary satisfaction, our purpose brings lasting contentment.

....

Read and discuss: *Hebrews 13:5 and 1 Thessalonians 5:16–18*
What do these passages say about contentment and purpose?

Windows and mirrors

....

But many who are first will be last, and the last first.
—Mark 10:31 NIV

A PASTOR FRIEND RECENTLY SHARED WITH ME one of his latest sermon illustrations. He related that he had asked his congregation if they were looking at the world through a mirror or a window. The implications are obvious, but no matter how evident the question's intent, it is one worth repeating again and again.

It is all too easy for us to crowd the proverbial mirror until those around us become nothing more than peripheral distractions. Consumed with our personal agendas, we quickly lose sight of everyone else, even those closest to us. Without even realizing it, we push people away and deny ourselves the joy of fellowship. Becoming increasingly self-absorbed, we fuel not only our selfishness, but bitterness, fear, and insecurity.

In a world that encourages us to look out for number one, Jesus calls us to another standard. He calls us to deny ourselves and follow Him and His example of putting others' needs above our own.

In Matthew 20:20–28, the mother of James and John asked Jesus to allow her sons to sit one on each side of Him when He reigns in His eternal Kingdom. Jesus responded by telling her, "You don't know what you are asking." He went on to say, "… whoever wants to be first must be your slave …" Certainly not the sentiment of one looking too closely at their own reflection.

....

Read and discuss: *Matthew 20:20–28*

What do you think about the mother's request?

Have you ever asked God for something out of selfish motives?

How does the world's view of success differ from the definition found in Scripture?

The gentle whisper

*You will seek Me and find Me when you seek Me
with all your heart.*

—Jeremiah 29:13 NIV

WHAT DOES IT MEAN TO SEEK GOD with all your heart? In a world full of noise and distractions, few things receive our full attention. We are constantly distracted by tweets and texts, not to mention all of life's normal responsibilities and obligations.

In 1 Kings 19:9–18, the prophet Elijah was holed up in a cave fearing for his life when God spoke to him saying, "… go out and stand on the mountain in the presence of the Lord, for the Lord is about to pass by." Elijah then witnessed a great and powerful wind, followed by an earthquake and fire, but God was in none of these. Instead, Elijah heard the voice of God in a gentle whisper.

Why a whisper? He is God after all—why not crashes of thunder and flashes of lightening with all the fanfare you might expect from the Creator of the universe? Because God does not desire pomp and circumstance—He desires our heart. We can hear the thunder as we cower in a corner, and an authoritative bellow can make us turn away. But a whisper, that requires our full, undivided attention, tuning out all else as we strain to hear the voice of God, focusing fully on His face, studying even the most subtle movement of His lips.

Try this sometime when sharing something important, soften your voice to a whisper and watch those to whom you speak, raise their heads and fix their eyes full on your face.

In a world of almost constant noise and distractions, it is imperative that we take time to be still (Psalm 37:7 and 46:10) and listen for God's gentle whisper.

Discuss:
In what ways might you begin to practice the discipline of being still?

Comparison

....

When Peter saw him, he asked, "Lord, what about him?"
—John 21:21 NIV

COMPARISON, I BELIEVE, SKEWS OUR SELF-PERCEPTION more than nearly anything else. In it, there are no redeeming qualities: either we puff ourselves up (causing a false sense of security and inflated pride), or we fall prey to hopelessness and frustrations, which abound in the hearts of those who continually underestimate their value. In either case, the results are the same: potential squelched, if not rendered altogether useless.

We may look at the neighbor's twenty year old car, their weed-infested flower bed, or protruding midsection, and feel pretty good about ourselves. Then again, if we peer across the lawn in the other direction, we may observe another neighbor enjoying his fancy pool while his late model sports car glistens in the sun and immediately feel inadequate. Suddenly, our grass is not as green, our house offers no solace, and our car is just something to drive.

True contentment begins with an accurate view of oneself. Realizing we fall short of God's glory (Romans 3:23) will help keep us humble, while praising God for His saving grace and amazing love. Understanding we are continually at the front of God's mind (Psalm 139:17–18) reminds us our value is not dependant upon what we possess, and knowing when we are living out our purpose (Ephesians 2:10) there is no reason for us to rob God of His glory by taking undue credit or to be envious of others for their apparent success. When we are tempted to compare, we need only to remember God created each of us uniquely; we are a one of a kind, not an assembly line replica.

....

Discuss:
The trappings of comparison and the freedom of finding our identity in Christ.

The beauty of waiting

But those who wait on the LORD shall renew their strength;
they shall mount up with wings like eagles ...

—Isaiah 40:31 NKJV

"WAITING..." AS CLASSIC ROCKER TOM PETTY SAYS in his song, "The Waiting", "... is the hardest part."[22] We do not like to wait ... on anything. We pace in front of microwaves, look repeatedly at our watch as we sit in the drive-through, and fidget in the pew if our pastor's sermon runs long. Often, it seems when God calls us to something, He necessarily requires of us a time of preparation, where our passions are refined, our resolve is tested, and ... we wait.

Abraham and Sarah waited for their son, Joseph waited in a prison cell, and the apostle Paul—following his conversion—spent three years in the wilderness before beginning his ministry.

Waiting can try us, but it also strengthens us. In waiting we are sifted and forged, our skills sharpened, and our commitment cemented. Ultimately, it is the proving of the wilderness experience which ensures we have the endurance needed to finish the race. Waiting is a difficult but necessary part of the process. It is, as Scripture tells us, a blessing. "Yes the LORD longs to be gracious to you; He rises to show you compassion. For the LORD is a God of justice. Blessed are all who wait for Him" (Isaiah 30:18).

Discuss:

What challenges are experienced as we wait?

Can you recall a time when you were waiting in a wilderness?

How, as described in Isaiah 30:18, can waiting be a blessing?

You deserve *what?*

....

*For the wages of sin is death, but the gift of God
is eternal life through Christ Jesus our LORD.*
—*Romans 6:23 NIV*

THE AVERAGE AMERICAN IS BOMBARDED with 3,000 advertisements per day, according to fluiddrivemedia.com,[23] and most, it seems, appeal to our selfish nature, more often than not telling us what we *deserve*. This speaks to the attitude of entitlement, prevalent in our culture.

If we have been hurt in an accident we deserve an exorbitant settlement, we deserve to be pampered, we deserve a vacation, and the list goes on, but what does the Bible say?

We are, as a result of the fall, born with original sin. While we did not have a choice in this matter, sin is, nonetheless, part of the human condition, which makes us deserving of only one thing: death.

Fortunately, God does not deal with us according to what we deserve (Psalm 103:10), but according to the grace afforded us by Jesus' sacrificial death on the cross. And unlike anything those 3,000+ advertisements have to offer, God's grace will never break, wear out, or become obsolete.

....

Read and discuss: *1 John 3:1–10*

What does this text say about our identity in Christ?

How does this differ from the messages we receive from the world?

How does our identity in Christ differ from that which we deserve?

Normal is overrated

....

> *… If I were still trying to please men,*
> *I would not be a bond-servant of Christ.*
>
> *—Galatians 1:10 NASB*

IT SEEMS A GREAT MANY PEOPLE desire normalcy. They concern themselves with what others think, how they dress, and what they drive. While keeping up with the Jones' may motivate some, it is anything but healthy, leading to an inaccurate sense of self-worth, and unhealthy stressors like unnecessary debt and a false sense of security, which is evidenced by our dependence on something other than our relationship with God.

It is easy to look to society, peers, or our industry for validation, but in doing so, we overlook an important truth: Our validation comes not from men but from our Heavenly Father.

I am quite sure God is not in the least bit concerned with normalcy. If He were, the stories of most of our biblical heroes would have been lost to history. Noah, after all, was the butt of the joke for a hundred years—building an ark on dry land (Genesis 6 and 7); David, being the youngest, was not even summoned from the field when Samuel came to anoint one of Jesse's sons King (1 Samuel 16:1–13); John the Baptist wore camel hair and had a regular diet of locusts and wild honey (Matthew 3:4); Ezekiel laid on his side for 390 days and ate food baked over a dung-fueled fire (Ezekiel 4); Hosea married an unfaithful prostitute (Hosea 1–3); and the list goes on.

When God calls us, He instructs us to count the cost, to be willing to give up everything, including our desire to fit in.

....

Read and discuss: *John 6:25–71* and *Galatians 1:10*

Talk about a time when you had to deny yourself in order to follow Christ.

What were the consequences?

The blessings?

Have you ever struggled to win approval?

How did this make you feel?

Lamp unto my feet

....

Your word is a lamp for my feet, a light on my path.
—*Psalm 119:105 NIV*

WHEN I WAS A BOY, I would sometimes go 'coon hunting with my dad. Raccoons are usually nocturnal, so they are hunted at night, and my job was to carry the kerosene lantern. As we walked through the fields and woods, the lantern provided just enough light to see a few feet in either direction.

As I think back to the lantern dangling in my hand, I am reminded of Psalm 119:105 and the comparison of God's word to a lamp for our feet. Though we sometimes wish we could have a spotlight into the future, God provides for us, through His Word, just enough light for the next few steps. I sometimes wonder if we were to actually see a far distance down the path what our response might be. Would we veer off in another direction, turn back, or at the very least drag our feet to the point we never go as far as we had originally intended?

I can recall times in my own life when, had I known what lie ahead, I would have certainly tried to find another way. However, it is those very instances, those same times of struggle and angst, which I now recognize as having been needed to test my commitment and strengthen my resolve. Having just enough light to see only a few feet ahead affords us the luxury of focusing only on what is next. Free of distant distractions, we are able to walk with cautious courage, not because we are relying on our own strength, but—like that little boy with the lantern—because we know our Father is with us.

....

Read and discuss: *Matthew 6:25–34 and Psalm 23*
Discuss the contrasting emotions of a life of faith and one of worry.

Tapestry

....

For just as the body is one and has many members,
and all the members of the body, though many, are one body,
so it is with Christ.

—1 Corinthians 12:12 ESV

ATAPESTRY IS MADE UP OF MANY THREADS, woven into patterns or pictures. I marvel at the artistry of the weaver: the vision and patience. The required attentiveness alone is admirable, and the talent needed to transfer that which is seen only in the mind's eye to the loom is truly amazing.

While each thread is important to the whole of the tapestry, if one were to snag, it would be easier to clip it off rather than weave it back into the cloth. If the displaced thread were allowed to remain, it would not only serve as a noticeable distraction but also compromise even more threads. So it is with us, each being one thread in God's tapestry, making up a small part of the Body of Christ.

Our lives are meant to—in our own small way—reflect the image of Christ to those with whom we come in contact.

When we think too highly of ourselves, become self-conscious, or feign humility, we serve only as a distraction, much like the snagged thread. Our goal in this life is not to be the object of attention. Rather, our goal as the Church—the Bride of Christ—is to serve alongside fellow believers, providing for the world a glimpse of Jesus. If individually we become the focus, we serve not as an enhancement, but as a distraction to the cause of Christ. However, when viewed as intended, all traces of individual threads disappear in the magnificence, which is the image of Jesus Messiah, our Redeemer.

....

Read and discuss: *John 14:9–14*
How are others able to *see the Father* in us?

Rest

....

> *Six days do your work, but on the seventh day do not work,*
> *so that your ox and your donkey may rest, and so that the slave*
> *born in your household and the foreigner living among you*
> *may be refreshed.*
>
> —*Exodus 23:12 NIV*

I N OUR FAST PACED, always-get-ahead, over-stimulated society, rest is often viewed as a novelty, an inhibitor of our to-do list or a missing rung on the corporate ladder. But rest is a gift.

For the 400 years prior to the Exodus, the Israelites were slaves, working seven days a week, 365 days a year. All they knew was work, but when God brought the Hebrew people out of Egypt, He gave them the gift of rest in the form of the Sabbath.

Sabbath rest not only provides time to refresh but also time to enjoy relationships with friends and family. And of course the Sabbath also allows us time to celebrate the blessings of our relationship with God through corporate worship.

By the time Jesus arrived on the scene, the Pharisees had taken the day meant as a gift and turned it into one more burdensome commandment. Jesus however, made the Father's intent clear in Mark 2:27 when He said, "The Sabbath was made for man, not man for the Sabbath." And as scripture tells us, "… His commands are not burdensome." (1 John 5:3).

God's commands are not meant to weigh us down but to free us. Free us from slavery to anything: fashion, career, addiction, approval, legalism, fear, pride or any of the many other, sometimes subtle things which can ensnare us and keep us from living out our God-given purpose in freedom.

....

Read and discuss: *1 John 5:2–4*

Why is it sometimes difficult to rest?

Are there adjustments you need to make to your schedule in order to enjoy the gift of the Sabbath?

You are not alone

....

There is therefore now no condemnation to those who
are in Christ Jesus, who do not walk according to the flesh,
but according to the Spirit.

—Romans 8:1 NKJV

O NE OF THE GREATEST FEARS of any human is simply to be alone. To have no one who cares, no one who understands, no one with whom you can share joys or sorrows, or just a good laugh.

It is possible to be surrounded by people and yet feel all alone: a slave to your fears and a prisoner to your secrets. I believe isolation is one of our enemy's most effective tools.

I have heard many stories of people who have carried burdens they could not bring themselves to share until they were on their death bed. Maybe it is the pain of a past mistake, the wounds of angry words or actions they have allowed to define them, or simply circumstances beyond their control, but whatever the case, these burdens have kept the individual locked away in a virtual solitary confinement, a prisoner of their fear and shame.

When opportunities arise that may afford fellowship and freedom, words of fear and doubt threaten any hope of betterment, keeping those held captive from venturing beyond their invisible walls. Walls, deceptively thick, but only able to provide a false sense of familiar security, while simultaneously affirming their lies, condemning their victim to a life of increasing hopelessness. But Jesus came to break down walls and set the captives free, and His freedom is available to all who call on His name.

....

Read: *Deuteronomy 31:6* and *Psalm 27:10*

Discuss:

Are there past mistakes you continue to allow to define you?

Does low self-esteem or the perception of others dictate your actions or inactions?

Have you ever found yourself struggling to be *good enough*?

Is there any situation or circumstance in which you feel alone?

Take the plunge!

....

> *God is our refuge and strength, an ever-present help in trouble.*
> *Therefore we will not fear, though the earth give way and the*
> *mountains fall into the heart of the sea, though its waters roar*
> *and foam and the mountains quake with their surging.*
> —*Psalm 46:1-3 NIV*

I HAVE NEVER BEEN THE BEST SWIMMER. While I am able to get from one side of a pool to the other, my flailing would never be considered even remotely graceful.

Before I could swim, water frightened me. When others my age were jumping off the diving boards, I was hanging out in the kiddie pool. And if I were to somehow muster enough courage to find my way into the "big pool," my confidence was only as strong as the death-grip I held on the pool's edge.

One evening, when I was probably seven or eight years old, my entire family went to the pool, which was a rare treat. We had not been there long when my dad set his sites on coaxing me into the big pool. After repeatedly assuring me he would not let me sink, I finally took a deep breath and jumped. Just as the water engulfed my entire body, my dad's hands were there lifting me up. I quickly grabbed the edge of the pool, pulled myself out, and jumped back into his arms. The water, that only moments earlier had been a source of great anxiety, now provided me with immense joy. It was still just as deep, but the knowledge that my dad was there to catch me eliminated all my fears and dismissed all my objections. In the absence of fear, I soon learned to swim.

While our earthly fathers cannot always be there to catch us, we can rest assured that if our Heavenly Father is calling us to something, He will be.

....

Discuss:
The correlation between faith and action.

Shame says "wear it," grace says "forget it"

We have seen His glory, the glory of the one and only Son,
who came from the Father, full of grace and truth.

—John 1:14 NIV

SET IN 17TH CENTURY PURITAN BOSTON, Nathaniel Hawthorne's classic, *The Scarlet Letter*,[24] tells the story of Hester Prynne, a woman who conceives a daughter through an adulterous affair. Because of her sin and unwillingness to reveal the name of her lover, Hester is forced to wear a scarlet *A* as an ever-present reminder of her shame.

Though such a punishment is unheard of in 21st century America, social stigmas, lasting consequence, and internal turmoil can haunt us for a lifetime, relegating us to a life of shame and regret. While there may be no visible signs of guilt, beneath the surface, our hearts can languish in a constant state of angst.

While shame says, "wear it, cling to it, and own it," fortunately our Judge willingly extends to all who will receive it, the grace for which our wounded souls so desperately long. One of the starkest examples of this is found in John chapter 8.

While Jesus was teaching, the Pharisees and teachers of the law brought before Him a woman caught in the act of adultery. Citing the Law of Moses, they were prepared to stone her to death. Before commencing the execution, however, they asked Jesus His thoughts. His reply: "If any one of you is without sin, let him be the first to throw a stone at her." When her accusers had gone, Jesus told her He also did not condemn her and then said, "Go now and leave your life of sin." No shame, no scarlet letter, no forfeiture of her life—just grace.

Read and discuss: John 8:1–11

Have you ever found it difficult to accept or receive forgiveness?

Have you ever experienced the burden of unforgiveness or the freedom of authentic forgiveness?

Vulnerable

....

*Then the man and his wife heard the sound of the L*ORD *God as He was walking in the garden in the cool of the day, and they hid from the L*ORD *God among the trees ...*

—*Genesis 3:8 NIV*

BEFORE THE FALL, everything was perfect. Perfect fellowship, perfect peace, and perfect health. But once sin entered the world everything changed. Chaos not only became the new normal in the form of pain, fear, and death, but for the first time, Adam and Eve felt a very real sense of vulnerability. Sin brought with it a keen understanding of danger and an awareness of the adversary. Before the fall, they knew only goodness, but with sin came an immediate and heartbreaking knowledge of evil, complete with all its trappings.

This awareness drove Adam and Eve to sew fig leaves together to cover their nakedness, but I believe this was much more than simple modesty. The fig leaves represented not only an attempt to clothe themselves but also an effort to mask their insecurities. Sin makes us feel shame, and shame is always accompanied by insecurity and self-consciousness, which naturally encourages us to hide.

Our fig leaves can assume many forms: not only the latest fashions but our careers, our cliques, or countless other status symbols which offer a type of covering. But, beyond the fig leaves, we are prone to a much more dangerous response: we hide. Our insecurities, brought about by our sin and our sin nature (original sin) will, if allowed, drive us from the presence of God. The good news is that Jesus broke the bond of sin and death and took upon Himself our shame so that we can approach God with confidence, not because of our goodness, but because of His.

....

Consider:

In what ways might you be tempted to hide from God?

The gift

....

For God so loved the world, that He gave His only begotten Son,
that whoever believes in Him shall not perish, but have eternal life.

—John 3:16 NASB

WHEN I WAS A CHILD, probably the most well known and oft' quoted Bible verse was John 3:16. What a great promise! What an amazing hope! Eternal life availed to us all.

Though I could easily quote this verse and adamantly professed it as truth, I still found myself fearful of God. And while totally inconsistent with the faith I espoused, I was much more aware of my fear than of the peace afforded me through His sacrifice.

While the good news is clearly communicated in today's verse, God does not stop there. He continues to affirm His promise in verse seventeen, "For God did not send the Son into the world to judge the world, but that the world might be saved through Him." Another translation uses the word *condemn* in place of *judge*.

Yet, because I knew I was unworthy of grace, I still found myself fearful of judgment and condemnation. I just could not wrap my mind around the beauty and peace of unconditional love. Had I not just memorized John 3:16, but clung to the truth it so clearly communicates, I could have spared myself a great deal of anxiety.

While God will judge those who choose not to follow His Son, His desire is for none to perish. God, knowing our need for a Savior, made a way. A way chosen, not earned; a way of Love and Peace, not fear and condemnation.

....

Read and discuss: Romans 5:15–17 and Romans 8:1–2
Why is it difficult to sometimes accept love without condition and grace without tribute?

A life of freedom and purpose

....

*Now faith is confidence in what we hope for
and assurance about what we do not see.*

—Hebrews 11:1 NIV

*God surpasses our dreams when we reach past our
personal plans and agenda to grab the hand of Christ
and walk the path He chose for us. He is obligated to
keep us dissatisfied until we come to Him and His plan
for complete satisfaction.*

—Beth Moore, Breaking Free: Discover
the Victory of Total Surrender[25]

*To love means loving the unlovable.
To forgive means pardoning the unpardonable.
Faith means believing the unbelievable.
Hope means hoping when everything seems hopeless.*

—G.K. Chesterton[26]

Dream come true

....

For we are God's masterpiece. He has created us anew
in Christ Jesus, so we can do the good things He planned
for us long ago.

—Ephesians 2:10 NLT

THROUGHOUT MY CHILDHOOD and well into my adult years, I was often lulled to sleep by a reoccurring dream, which, though always a comfort, seemed to me to be of little relevance. Consequently, I never shared my dream with anyone until after a brief meeting with the band *100 Portraits*. I do not have enough space to share with you what led to that opportunity, but I can tell you it was something only God could orchestrate.

Through much of my life, fear was a constant companion. It dictated my thoughts and squelched my joy, until that not-so-chance encounter—Palm Sunday, 2007.

As the band was preparing to leave, they gathered around me to pray. Then, someone from the band shared a vision she said God had given her. She went on to describe my dream in perfect detail, but what she said next was even more amazing. "This is from your Heavenly Father," she said. "He says this vision has always been a comfort to you and it means you are free to be the person you were created to be. Now walk in that freedom."

For the first time in my life I felt the permission to be me. What freedom, what peace, what purpose!

But this dream is not uniquely mine. The same message is meant for *all* of us. God has created each of us for a unique purpose and I am convinced true freedom is only found when we are walking in it.

....

Discuss:

Is there anyone close to you from whom you have never received affirmation?

How has this affected your life?

How might the verse above speak to you?

The real deal

....

*For what will it profit a man if he gains the whole world
and forfeits his soul?*

—*Matthew 16:26 NASB*

IN A CULTURE IMMERSED IN THE SUPERFICIAL, people are judged by their looks, weight, clothes, car, house, company they keep—the list goes on. But, even to those who attain most or all of what culture deems desirable, happiness can still prove elusive.

With a nice house in Nashville, a record deal, hit songs, and admiration, Rich Mullins had what culture would call a successful career. But he gave it all away to serve the Navajo on the Window Rock Indian Reservation in New Mexico. He paid himself a blue-collar salary and gave the rest of his earnings to charity. He spent the last years of his life denying himself the comforts of the "American Dream," choosing instead to serve others. He lived a life, not of perfection, but of transparency and total abandon to God and people. I think this side of Rich might be best summed up in a line from his song "If I Stand" in which he sings: "The stuff of Earth competes for the allegiance I owe only to the Giver of all good things."[27] Rich obviously held to a very healthy attitude toward the temporal.

Another songwriter, who honestly sings of the struggle to be transparent, is Andy Gullahorn. In his song "I Haven't Either," he sings: "Have you ever felt compelled to get a weight off of your chest, but can't follow through because you are ashamed? I've heard that you can tell the ones who truly open up, their lives are marked with freedom and with peace …"[28]

Freedom and peace: the fruits of transparency.

....

Discuss:

Are there things in your life keeping you from trusting God enough to be completely His?

Are you tempted to live up to the expectations of others?

Who do you look to for validation?

We all have a story

....

… I was going to Damascus …

—*Acts 26:12 NIV*

I STILL REMEMBER MANY OF THE BIBLE VERSES I learned as a boy in Sunday school. The truths they hold have continued to provide me with benefits which have long outlasted the candy rewards I received for their memorization. To understand the importance of having Scripture "hidden in our heart," we have to look no further than the example of Jesus in the wilderness resisting temptation with Scriptural truth—even in a time of extreme vulnerability.

But as important as Scripture is to our life, many times the most effective way to witness to our faith is simply to learn to communicate our story.

Many times the thought of sharing our faith can be quite intimidating, but when we are able to honestly share our fears and struggles, our transparency provides a platform on which we are best able to communicate the hope that has set us free.

After all, the world is seldom impressed with the number of Scriptures we are able to quote, but a man of honest transparency can gain not only their attention but also their respect.

A friend of mine who is a national recording artist once told me he spends more time rehearsing his story than his songs. Anyone can sing Christian songs, but it is in the stories of God's faithfulness to us we can most passionately and effectively communicate humanity's need for a Savior.

....

Read: *Acts 26*
Notice how Paul used his story to share the Gospel.

Exercise:
Take time to consider your story; in doing so, do not yield to the temptation to dismiss it as boring or inconsequential. If you struggle to recognize anything worth sharing, ask someone close to you for their honest observations about God's work in your life.

You just don't know it yet

....

... those He called, He also justified ...
—Romans 8:30 NIV

VALIDATION CAN COME FROM THE STRANGEST PLACES. I think God gets our attention the most when we expect it the least. One such instance in my life came as God was beginning to stir my heart for things of ministry.

One day I found myself at a business I used to frequent, owned by a very nice lady about the same age as my mother. She was one of those people who always seemed to need to talk, and it was seldom just light-hearted chit-chat. She was not at all negative, though she frequently dealt with her share of drama, and being a self-professed agnostic, she had no faith to bring her solace. So you can imagine my surprise when, during one of our conversations, she looked at me and said, "You are such a good minister." This was a year or so before my music ministry began, and at that time I had no inkling I would ever be in ministry (though looking back, it is now clear God was preparing me for that very purpose). In my surprise, I responded, "I'm not a minister." Smiling, she replied, "Yes you are, you just don't know it yet."

Many times, I believe, we resist God's call, not out of fear, or unwilling-ness to sacrifice, but out of a sense of unworthiness. Fortunately, we have the truth of Scripture to quell our self-doubt, and often it is reinforced in unlikely ways.

....

Read and discuss: Romans 8:28–39

Have you struggled to respond to God's call on your life?

What assurances are offered in this text?

What encouragement do you find in these verses?

Have you ever experienced God speaking to you through an unlikely person or circumstance?

Are You a Seeker?:
A second look at Luke 19:10

[Jesus came] to seek and to save the lost.

—Luke 19:10 ESV

S EVERAL YEARS AGO, my former church was experiencing a significant growth spurt. Suddenly, both young Christians and seekers alike were numbered among our regulars. Our church was small and off the beaten path so, in light of the new growth and in the hope of drawing more people to our church, and ultimately to Christ, I suggested we look into some advertising, to which one of the elders replied, "They know we're here, this church has been in the same spot for 150 years!"

Unfortunately such sentiments speak more to a fear of discomfort or a lack of vision than to a genuine concern for the lost. We often hear of churches being "seeker friendly," but this often just implies an acceptance of those who know they are lost and stop in to ask for directions. What if we expanded upon that to include a congregation willing to go into the highways and byways, the back alleys and public places to seek the lost?

To model Christ we need to be both seekers of the *truth* and seekers of the *lost*. Waiting for people to darken the doorsteps of our church buildings, with or without an ad campaign, will never be as effective as having a congregation of believers burdened enough for the lost to meet them where they are, even if it means getting our hands dirty or immersing ourselves in situations where we may feel a little out of our element.

Read and discuss: *Luke 15:1–10*

How did the people in these parables respond when realizing something they valued was lost?

How did the same people respond upon finding their lost possession?

What do these passages say about God's attitude toward the lost?

How should our attitudes mirror His?

Eat your veggies!

....

> *... God hath chosen the weak things of the world*
> *to confound the things which are mighty ...*
>
> —*1 Corinthians 1:27 NKJV*

IT IS A VERY HUMAN THING to desire to lighten our load, yield to the temptation to take the easy way out, or at the very least, allow our perception of those whom we believe to "have it better" somehow affect our mood and validate our insecurities.

If you homeschool, you may worry your child is missing something by not having access to all of the resources available in the public or private schools. If you attend a small church, you may wonder if things would be better in a mega church with its dynamic programs and technology. Or perhaps you are a stay-at-home mom who sometimes feels as though your role is somehow less significant because you are not bringing home a pay check. The key, of course, is not about being the biggest, the best, or having the most—if that were the case, God would have never called David, Gideon, or any one of the apostles.

There are several more "least of these" biblical heroes I could mention, but I believe Daniel chapter 1 provides a perfect example of the blessings of faithfulness. Forsaking the temptation to yield to pressures which would compromise their faith, Daniel, Hananiah, Mishael, and Azariah chose a diet of vegetables and water, over the delicacies of the king. In the end, God honored their obedience with wisdom and favor.

....

Read and discuss: *Daniel 1*

What did Daniel and the others risk by not following the king's diet?

What benefit did they gain because of their obedience?

Have you ever sacrificed immediate benefits or approval in order to follow your call?

In what areas of your life might you struggle with the desire to take the easy way out?

How might these types of situations affect your life?

Good Friday

....

God made Him who had no sin to be sin for us,
so that in Him we might become the righteousness of God.
—2 Corinthians 5:21 NIV

A S I WRITE THIS, it is Good Friday morning, the day I would consider the second most important in our faith, the first of course being Easter or Resurrection Sunday. The longer I live, the more I am truly amazed by God's plan and the extent to which He would go to make it possible for us to have a relationship with Him.

We learn early in our Christian faith the truth reflected in the verse above, but what does it mean to *become* sin for us? In Ephesians chapter five, we read that Jesus gave Himself up for the Church in order to "present her to Himself as a radiant church, without stain or wrinkle or any other blemish, but holy and blameless." As part of the Church, The Bride of Christ, Jesus views us the same way, "without stain or wrinkle," while He bears the scars rightfully our own.

It is one thing to have someone pay our debt, it is quite another to consider the scars willingly borne by the Resurrected Christ. Scars which make it possible for Him to look upon us as *radiant and without blemish.*

Tony Campolo describes Jesus, when on the cross, as being suspended not just between earth and Heaven, but between past and future, existing in the "instantaneous now."[29] At that moment He is reaching into days long past and those yet to come, including this very moment, pulling our sin onto Himself. This is the source of our radiance and the reason for our freedom.

....

Discuss:

What does it look like to love as Christ loves, in our homes, churches and communities?

Talk about forgiveness and any opportunities you have to extend it to others.

We're farmers too

....

I tell you the truth, anyone who gives you a cup of water
in My name because you belong to Christ will certainly not
lose his reward.
—Mark 9:41 NIV

IN MARCH OF 2012, Southern Indiana, Kentucky and Tennessee were struck by devastating tornados. In the days and weeks that followed, aide poured into the communities in the form of supplies and manpower. Our family was part of the relief effort joining twenty-five other volunteers from our community who traveled to southern Indiana to assist with the clean up.

The first day we were assigned to help a farmer whose fields were littered with downed trees and debris. Before we began our work, he spoke with us about the tornado and the land which had belonged to his family for generations. As he talked about the fields, which would soon need to be prepared for spring planting, he struggled to hold back tears. Just then, one of several farmers in our group spoke up and simply said, "We're farmers too." Now I was choking back tears. To say anything else seemed quite unnecessary. The amount of compassion, support, and comfort communicated in those few words spoke volumes.

We often look for any reason to avoid uncomfortable situations because we do not know what to say. But love does not require even a single spoken word. Compassion and concern sometimes are best accompanied by simple acts of service, a caring embrace, or a heartfelt prayer.

As we read in today's verse, even simply providing a cup of cold water can be a blessing.

....

Discuss:
Have you ever experienced God's presence when serving others?
Is there someone who needs your help today?

Are you called to lead?

....

> *But Moses said to God, "Who am I that I should go to Pharaoh and bring the Israelites out of Egypt?*
>
> —*Exodus 3:11 NIV*

I ONCE HEARD STEVE BROWN, radio host of *Key Life*, tell his audience that if they found confrontation enjoyable, they were not called to do it. I think the same could be said of leadership.

I am not one who relishes the responsibility of leadership. It would be easier for me to sit back and take direction from someone more qualified rather than take charge, but sometimes I find myself in positions where I am called to lead.

Moses was another reluctant leader. Why? Because he was more focused on his weakness than on God's strength. That is a clear indication we somehow believe our shortcomings and insecurities are greater than God's strength and ability.

Just as God reminded Paul in 2 Corinthians 12, so must we at times be reminded, "My power is made perfect in weakness …" So how does this work? When we know we do not possess the strength, skills, or foresight to accomplish the task at hand, we must necessarily rely on God to make up the difference. Not only will this dependence help us stay close to Him, but it will also keep us from so easily taking credit for what He has done through us.

Sometimes I have to remind myself that God equips those He calls. When feeling unqualified for a particular task, I simply need to remember my confidence rests not in my own strength or ability, but in the God whom I serve.

....

Read and discuss: *Romans 12:8 and Matthew 20:28*

What do these verses say about leadership?

Are you a leader in your career, church, or home?

Consider the characteristics of Jesus as a servant leader.

By the roots

....

... where the Spirit of the Lord is, there is freedom.

—2 Corinthians 3:17 NIV

ONE OF THE MOST BASIC OF HUMAN DESIRES is the desire to be free. It is for this reason we remember the lives of men and women throughout history who have defended the cause of liberty. Movies are made, books are written, and monuments are erected in their honor. Yet, while the masses desire freedom, tyrants will, if the opportunity permits, conquer all within their reach in an attempt to quench their insatiable thirst for power and control.

Similarly, there are spiritual tyrants which can lie deep beneath the surface, seeking to control our spirit—robbing us of joy and holding our freedom hostage.

I recently heard that the most common of these tyrants threatening Christians today is bitterness. In and of itself this is problematic, but the troubles are often compounded by the fact that bitterness is usually accompanied by resentment, chronic anger, and the desire for revenge, all of which, I believe, are by-products of unforgiveness.

The bitter root grows deep and, consequently is difficult to extract. However, when we remove the visible without also dealing with what lies beneath the surface, bitterness will continue to exist and—like a power-hungry tyrant with free reign—ultimately claim more of our heart as its own.

We often feel a right to our offense, and though we may be justified in our anger, I have found true forgiveness to be the key to a life of freedom, both in receiving it for ourselves and extending it to others.

....

Read and discuss: *Ephesians 4:31–32*

Who is on your doorstep?

....

> *... at his gate was laid a beggar named Lazarus ...*
> —Luke 16:20 NIV

I N HIS BOOK, *The Hole in Our Gospel*,[30] World Vision president Rich Strearns expounds upon the parable of the rich man and Lazarus the beggar. He makes a piercing observation, which I had—until I read this book—overlooked. I always pictured Lazarus crawling up to a random home and waiting for the owner to pass by, but as Rich points out, the verb used in this parable is *laid*. Someone deliberately placed Lazarus on this particular step, specifically because they knew the rich man had the means with which to help. Lazarus had obviously been a regular occupant of this same step, because the rich man knew his name. It is this nugget of information which leads to a more personal question: Who has God placed upon your doorstep?

Maybe this is literally someone who shows up at your door, maybe it is someone who is often brought to the front of your mind, or perhaps a person or cultural group for whom you feel a particular burden. So often we think of ministry in terms of traveling to the remotest jungles of Africa, but what about the single mother next door, the shut-in down the street, or the dirty-faced neighbor boy who just pulled up a fistful of your flowers?

....

Consider:

Who has God placed upon your doorstep?

What can you do to serve them with the love of Christ?

Note: One of the most tangible and satisfying things my family and I do is to sponsor three children through the ministry of World Vision. Our sponsorship provides opportunities for each of them to enjoy the benefits of clean water, regular meals, medical attention, education, spiritual nourishment and hope. If you would like more information on child sponsorship, please visit **WorldVision.FryeFamilyBand.net**.

The Great Mystery

Beyond all question, the Mystery from which true godliness springs is great: He appeared in the flesh, was vindicated by the Spirit, was seen by angels, was preached among the nations, was believed on in the world, was taken up in glory.

—1 Timothy 3:16 NIV

SEVERAL YEARS AGO, my family and I were part of a work team that traveled to the Standing Rock Indian Reservation in South Dakota. We helped with some small construction projects, did some painting, assisted with a Vacation Bible School, and spent time getting to know some of the people there—a few of whom have remained friends.

While on the reservation, I learned a hand full of Lakota words, including two for God. *Wakantanka*, which means *Big Holy* and *Taku Wakanke*, which is literally translated *The Big What Is It*, or more colloquially, *The Great Mystery*. When I heard this, I was struck by the fact that the apostle Paul used similar terminology in reference to Jesus: "My goal is that they may be encouraged in heart and united in love, so that they may have the full riches of complete understanding, in order that they may know the Mystery of God, namely, Christ in whom are hidden all the treasures of wisdom and knowledge" (Colossians 2:2-3). Paul's goal was also our goal for that week, but no matter whether we are on a mission trip miles from home or in our own hometown, our desire should be the same: that our lives may encourage others in order that they know Christ more deeply.

Read and discuss: *Colossians 2:1–5*
What are some ways you might be able to serve others?
How might your acts of service help others know *the Mystery of God*?

Loneliness

....

I have seen all the things that are done under the sun;
all of them are meaningless, a chasing after the wind.

—*Ecclesiastes 1:14 NIV*

W**E HAVE BEEN PRIVILEGED** to work with a lot of great people over the years: on the road, in the studio, and on stage. We have had so many wonderful experiences and a few, though memorable, are not numbered among our favorite musical moments.

One such event, which caught us by surprise, happened when we were scheduled to open four concerts for another artist. We were truly looking forward to this, but our anticipation quickly turned to disappointment as the artist let us know in no uncertain terms they were not happy about having to share the stage with us. While this was certainly awkward, we tried to make the best of it and hoped the audience would not pick up on the not-so-inconspicuous, tension.

The next day, as I considered the events of the previous night, my frustration turned to pity, as I realized the emptiness this artist must know. I was reminded of the book of Ecclesiastes—specifically, the verse which says all things are meaningless. I thought about the apparent cynicism, and then the nugget of truth lying just beneath the surface of the text—that being apart from God, everything *is* meaningless. Even the best this world has to offer will not bring happiness. It can't. But Christ brings meaning to even the most mundane routines of everyday life.

It was this experience which inspired our song "Loneliness," which says in part, "You've achieved all your hopes and dreams, but success ain't always what it seems. You've spent your life singing on the stage but tonight you entertain a guest called loneliness."[31]

....

Read and discuss: *Ecclesiastes 1*
What is the meaning of life?

No greater love

....

Greater love hath no man than this,
that a man lay down his life for his friends.

—John 15:13 ASV

LAST YEAR, WHILE IN SAN ANTONIO for a concert, I took a few hours to visit the Alamo. For me, this place is truly overwhelming. When soldiers go to war they know they are putting their lives on the line, but the Alamo was different. For these heroic freedom fighters, defending the Alamo and the liberties they held so dear meant, without a doubt, the forfeiture of their lives.

While Bowie and Crockett were celebrities of the day, most defenders were normal men, some native Texans, others recent immigrants, but all were committed to a purpose greater than themselves.

We often think of the phrase, "laying down our life" in terms of giving the ultimate sacrifice (and certainly that is a valid application), but one does not have to quit breathing in order to do so. Mother Teresa laid down her life while daily caring for lepers in Calcutta, George Mueller did the same for orphans in England, and Harriet Tubman spent years putting herself in harm's way to lead slaves to freedom. Jesus' words in Matthew 10:39 speak of men and women such as Mother Teresa, Mueller and Tubman; "… whoever loses his life for My sake will find it."

In life and in death, we lay down our lives when we live for a cause greater than ourselves. Serving others in the name of Jesus, caring for them with a love that necessitates sacrifice, and considering their comfort of greater importance than our own—that is the stuff true heroes are made of!

....

Read and discuss: *Matthew 10:24–42*
How are you called to lay down your life?
What challenges do you face because of it?

The unsettled life

....

Terah took his son Abram, his grandson Lot son of Haran,
and his daughter-in-law Sarai, the wife of his son Abram,
and together they set out from Ur of the Chaldeans to go to
Canaan. But when they came to Haran, they settled there.
Terah lived 205 years, and he died in Haran.

—*Genesis 11:31-32 NIV*

S EVERAL YEARS AGO I heard a minister say, "If you want to plan your life, God will let you, but if you want God to plan your life, you need to let go of your plans and follow Him." When I heard this I felt a wave of conviction and knew I needed to make some changes. As I began to pray for God to reveal to me any area of my life that was inconsistent with His plans, a whole series of things began to surface. I soon came to realize just how good of a planner I had become, due in large part to my efforts to build for myself and my family a safe and secure life.

While sharing with a friend my efforts to *un-plan* my life, I confessed I felt unsettled. His response: "That's a great place to be." He then pointed me to Genesis 11:31–32. He said it appeared from this text Terah was likely first called to the promised land and though he started out for Canaan, for some unknown reason he "settled" short of the goal. Abram would then eventually be called to the promised land and become known as the father of many nations. Those verses in Genesis have come to signify for me the importance of not allowing ourselves to feel too comfortable in this world and instead to trust God wherever He leads.

....

Read and discuss: *John 17:6–19*

What does it mean to be *in the world but not of the world*?

Do you have plans that are inconsistent with God's call on your life, or priorities that need to be reordered?

They really lived

....

... to live is Christ and to die is gain.

—*Philippians 1:21 NASB*

ONE OF MY ALL TIME FAVORITE MOVIES is *Second Hand Lions*.[32] It is the story of two bachelor brothers who find themselves in custody of their great nephew, Walter. Though living in a somewhat dilapidated farmhouse and appearing very back-woods, these adventurous uncles (though quite quirky) provide Walter with some much needed wisdom and stability. Throughout his teen years, Walter enjoys listening to his uncles' stories of war, travel, rescue, and lost love, which seem somewhat embellished if not altogether fabricated.

My favorite scene comes at the very end of the movie. Upon hearing of the death of these now elderly brothers, an oil tycoon from the Middle East arrives at the farmhouse with his son to pay his respects. After introducing himself to the now-adult nephew (played by Josh Lucas), the tycoon's son turns to his father and asks, "The men in Grandpa's stories really lived?" To which the smiling Walter replies, "Yeah, they *really* lived!"

Every time I watch this movie I am reminded to make the most of each moment, to live, live, live. It is so easy to surrender to the status quo, be taken captive by life's squeaky wheels, or simply become a spectator in the game of life, but these are not attitudes consistent with a life lived in Christ.

Jesus calls us to a life of purpose, which requires a heart in tune with God and a willingness to make deliberate decisions, in spite of circumstance, comfort, or popular opinion.

To *really live* is, as the apostle Paul said, Christ.

....

Read and discuss: *2 Thessalonians 3:5–7*
What does this passage say about deliberateness?
How does deliberateness and perseverance help us to "really live"?

Are you ready for an adventure?

....

I have come that they may have life, and have it to the full.
—John 10:10 NIV

YOU CAN BE QUITE SURE you will never see a movie billed as, "An average film, based on the boring life of a simple person in a sleepy one horse town." A script like that would never make it past the first reading. But if by some miracle it were to find its way to the big screen, it would most certainly be a bust.

We are drawn to movies with words like, "action-packed thriller full of drama and suspense," or "romantic comedy that will have you laughing long after the credits stop rolling." We all have our favorite genres, but certainly, we watch movies for one thing: to feel something—to stir our hearts, emotions, or passions.

We can, however, suffer some very negative consequences if we begin to transfer expectations of the glitz and glamour, the romance and adventure, or the fairy tail happy endings of the movies to our everyday, real life. And why should we? The Christian life is anything but boring.

Jesus calls us to take up our cross and follow Him. Our cross? That does not sound like much of an adventure, does it? It does if we consider that our cross is the very thing that brings meaning to our life. Our cross is not as much an instrument of death as it is the means through which we find our eternal purpose.

There is no man so free, as he who is willing to lay down his life for a cause greater than himself. Carrying our cross will almost certainly look a lot less like public execution, and more like a life of purpose. And that sounds like a greater adventure than any Hollywood make-believe.

....

Read and discuss: Mark 8:34–37
What do you think it means to lose your life for the sake of the Gospel?

I wish I could

Again, the kingdom of Heaven is like a merchant looking for fine pearls. When he found one of great value, he went away and sold everything he had and bought it.

—Matthew 13:45–46 NIV

HAVE YOU EVER FOUND YOURSELF SAYING, "I wish I could ..." fill in the blank. Play football like Peyton Manning, fiddle like Charlie Daniels, or maybe surf like Bethany Hamilton? I think if we are honest with ourselves we have all envied someone's talent at one time or another.

It is easy to be on the outside looking in and desire the perceived benefits of a particular skill. But talent alone is not enough. We envy the thrill of the win or the rush of the stage without consideration of the time, energy and sacrifice which led up to those few fleeting moments. "Success," as the old adage goes, "is where preparation and opportunity meet."

When we begin to view our purpose in light of the Kingdom, it is like finding the fine pearl referenced in Matthew 13. It affirms the necessity of our sacrifice and helps keep our victories in proper perspective: recognizing the joy of our success simply as a blessing—not the ultimate prize, and the world's validation (or lack thereof) as an inconsequential factor in our motivation.

Joseph would have never known the joy of leadership nor experienced its blessings were he not first sold into slavery and then wrongfully imprisoned. Looking back, Joseph certainly understood this difficult truth, and it was likely this understanding that allowed him to show such leadership and restraint.

Discuss:

Have you ever stopped to consider your purpose in Christ?

Is anything holding you back?

Are you willing to sacrifice everything to live it out?

The Gospel according to baseball

I have become all things to all people
so that by all possible means I might save some.

—*1 Corinthians 9:22 NIV*

W HEN I WAS YOUNG, I took piano lessons until I decided I would rather play sports. I worked hard, but soon discovered that, as an athlete, I was either the best of the worst or the worst of the best. And other than some non-competitive church softball, my sports career ended with high school.

Baseball is by far my favorite sport, and one day as I was watching a game I was struck with this analogy: *The Gospel is like baseball.* Now this may seem a stretch, but stay with me.

In order to win the World Series, a team must have many types of pitchers on its roster—left-handers, right-handers, starters, middle-relief, closers, fastball pitchers, finesse pitchers, etc.—many pitchers throwing the same ball in different ways to accomplish the same goal. And to take it one step further, if a pitcher is to have a long major league career, he will most likely have to adjust his delivery as his body ages, all the while continuing to throw the same ball: same size, same weight, same number of stitches.

I have seen churches thrive and others stagnate in direct correlation to their willingness to adjust their delivery. In the end however, our call is much higher than winning a World Series: our call has eternal ramifications. To put pride or personal preference above people, to make programs, musical styles, or any other issue a higher priority than the Gospel itself is idolatry.

Adjusting our delivery without compromising the truth—this is the example Christ gave us and one which is often required to reach others for Him.

Read and discuss: *1 Corinthians 9:21–23*

Your heart's desire

Delight yourself in the Lord and He will give you the desires of your heart.

—Psalm 37:4 NASB

Your heart's desire—have you ever thought about it? I mean really thought about it. Beyond the superficial, beneath the thin veneer of the latest fads and fashions, what is it your heart craves?

The Bible tells us in Ephesians 2:10, God created us for a purpose. "For we are God's workmanship, created in Christ Jesus to do good works, which God prepared in advance for us to do."

It is in these "good works" for which we were created, I believe, we find our heart's desire. But unfortunately, we often get bogged down trying to live up to cultural, familial or religious expectations, and in the process overlook, or at least greatly limit, our opportunities to live out our purpose.

I spent many years of my life simply pursuing goodness. In the process, I wasted a great deal of energy trying to please others while at the same time laboring to keep that which God had freely given: my salvation. In the end, my efforts only served to cloud my understanding and compete for my allegiance.

For this reason, when I began to feel a desire to pursue my passion of music, I quickly dismissed it as superficial, but God kept bringing it back until I finally relented.

So how do we delight ourselves in the Lord? How do we find our purpose? And how do we please God? I believe we accomplish all three when we press into Jesus to find our heart's desire, and then order our lives in such a way as to maximize our opportunities.

Read and discuss: *Hebrews 12:1–3*
How do these verses apply to the above text?

Expectancy

....

And when I am lifted up from the earth,
I will draw everyone to myself.

—John 12:32 NIV

"LIVE EXPECTING GOD TO BE AT WORK IN YOUR LIFE, but never put expectations on God." This is a motto I try to live by and also one with which I hope I have encouraged others. Over the years I have found that while God is always at work, He seldom works in ways we expect.

When living according to our expectations, we necessarily make life about us, limiting the ability for God to use us to further His Kingdom. However, when we seek God and His will, we find purpose and peace, many times, in spite of our expectations or those of others. This does not always translate into what anyone might consider "blessings," but God's plan affords a peace nothing else can provide.

Friends of ours from church had a dream of being missionaries. However, in the early years of their marriage a diagnosis of multiple sclerosis changed everything. While they never made it to the mission field, they spent years faithfully encouraging and supporting other missionaries who had. As long as I live I will never forget the amazing testimonies of God's goodness and faithfulness offered by this dear saint as she sat in her wheelchair, laboring to share words of praise and encouragement.

To me, her life will always serve as a reminder of faithfulness in spite of circumstance and trust without expectation.

....

Read and discuss: *Romans 8:18–27*

What are some ways you see creation "groaning" in anticipation?

In the same way, how might your spirit groan as you wait for adoption and redemption?

Has there been a time when you have put expectations on God?

How has He worked in, through, or around that situation?

Know where you are going

....

Where there is no vision, the people perish ...
—*Proverbs 29:18 KJV*

SEVERAL YEARS AGO, I received a great piece of advice which has continued to serve me well. The advice came in response to this question: "With all the different opportunities we receive in music ministry, how do we discern which to accept or pursue and which to decline?" The answer: "We first need to pray for God to reveal to us His vision and purpose for our life. Once we know this, we can simply evaluate each situation based not on what is most lucrative or impressive, but solely on what is consistent with our call. Not all great opportunities are right for us, and not all those less than desirable are wrong." That is some good stuff!

If people perish for lack of vision, then with it they are certain to thrive. Vision allows us to maximize our purposeful desires while at the same time eliminating any anxiety caused by second guessing. Vision also squelches the temptation to compare ourselves to others, allowing us to plunge headlong into our purpose.

It may require us to live in obscurity rather than the spotlight, or embrace frugality and deny ourselves the fleeting pleasures of creature comforts, but the benefits of the peace which vision affords always outweighs the temporal joys of the moment.

This truth is also reflected in something I was once told by a long time farmer: "My rows are always straight when I fix my eyes on something at the other end of the field."

....

Discuss:
What are the benefits of vision?
How does having a clear vision help in decision making?

107

Interpreting dreams

All the ways of a man are clean in his own sight, but the Lord weighs the motives. Commit your works to the Lord and your plans will be established.

—*Proverbs 16:2–3 NASB*

As I WRITE THIS, we are in Nashville for some meetings. It is hard to come here though, and not catch some live music.

Tonight we spent the evening at the Blue Bird Café and took in one of their open-mic nights. The talent pool on these evenings varies greatly—from artists just cutting their teeth, to those showcasing their seasoned skills—and tonight was no exception.

This city can be a great and yet cruel place. Some musicians are here living their dream, while others are spending every ounce of energy and more money than they have, simply chasing one.

Dreams can be hard to interpret, which sometimes makes it easy to mistake them for purpose. I believe God births within us passions meant to be used to serve His Kingdom. For many though, the only purpose served by chasing their dreams is their own. They either have not heard, or have chosen to ignore the peace and satisfaction availed them when submitting both their lives and dreams to the will of God.

For some here tonight, showcasing their talents, songwriting was simply a fun hobby and nothing more. For a few, it appeared a genuine gift that could potentially bring lifelong satisfaction and possible compensation. And for others, songwriting will continue to be a series of heartbreaks and frustrations. Why? Because they will spend the best years of their lives chasing a dream not theirs to live.

Discuss:

Are you living your dream or chasing one meant for someone else?

God has amazing plans for each of us, which will not always bring glamour, but will always provide purpose.

Comfort in the familiar

....

So if the Son sets you free, you are truly free.
—John 8:36 NLT

WHY DOES IT SOMETIMES SEEM EASIER to continue in a less than desirable situation rather than break free and change course? Chances are, if you have not been in this type of situation, you know of someone who has: choosing to remain in an abusive relationship, a dead end job, or stubbornly holding on to a bad attitude or habit. But why, when a better life is just one decision away?

I have often said, "There is comfort in the familiar even when the familiar isn't comfortable." We are creatures of habit, and ruts of course are created by habitually walking the same path. The longer we walk those familiar trails, the deeper the ruts become, and the deeper the ruts, the more difficult it is to break out of them.

Ultimately though, the reason we opt for the familiar is fear: fear of the uncomfortable, fear of the unknown, and as my pastor says, "Fear is the opposite of faith."

God does not call us to a life of comfort; He calls us to a life of purpose, and though not always comfortable, purpose affords us peace, which of course cannot coexist with fear.

Breaking free requires a deliberate effort to change course and a willingness to retrain our mind to focus, not on fear, but instead, on the truth of God's love, rejecting our own negative self-perceptions and bad habits and exchanging them for the loving acceptance and true purpose we only find as we walk with God.

....

Read and discuss: *1 John 4:18* and *Romans 8:1*

Are you allowing fear to control any areas of your life?

How, by surrendering our fears to God, can lies be replaced with truth and anxiety with peace?

About the author

The Frye family lives in a small rural Indiana town, where, as Tom says, they "simply do life together." From gardening and homeschooling to music ministry and daily chores, working together, playing together, and serving together have always been a part of the Frye family dynamic. It is through "doing life together" the Fryes have learned the importance of deliberateness, perseverance, and faith.

Tom and Lisa believe ministry begins at home; serving our spouses and our children. It is this understanding which led to the creation of the Family to Family event, which is designed to engage, equip and energize families to live out their God-given purpose.

Additionally, the Fryes are actively involved in ministry at Westchester United Methodist Church, where Tom is the Director of Contemporary Worship.

The Fryes are available for concerts, church services, homeschool and family events, as well as song writing and worship workshops. For more information on their music and ministry visit **FamilyFirstMinistries.net**.

Notes

Bible Versions used:

New American Standard Bible

New International Version

New Living Translation

The Message

English Standard Version

King James Version

New King James Version

American Standard Version

1. Ben Shive and Andrew Peterson, Andrew Peterson:
   Counting Stars (Centricity Music, ©2010 Andrew Peterson)

2. C.S. Lewis, *Mere Christianity*
   (New York: HarperCollinsPublishers, 2001), 52

3. Donald Miller, *Father Fiction: Chapters for a Fatherless Generation*
   (New York: Howard Books, 2010), 3

4. Polly House, "Want your church to grow? Then bring in the men,"
   Baptist Press. http://www.bpnews.net/bpnews.asp?id=15630.

5. Ralph Moody, *Little Britches* (New York: Norton, 1950) 36–42

6. Rainer Maria Rilke, *Quote by Rainer Maria Rilke: To love is good, too: love
   being difficult ...* , http://www.goodreads.com/quotes/84202-to-love-is-
   good-too-love-being-difficult-for-one

7. *Jerry Maguire.* Cameron Crowe, writer/director. TriStar Pictures 1996

8. Billy Graham, *Quote by Billy Graham: When wealth is lost ...* ,
   http://www.goodreads.com/quotes/653548-when-wealth-is-lost-nothing-is-
   lost-when-health-is

9. Matthew Warner, "Quote of the Day: Do it anyway [Mother Teresa]"
   Fallible Blogma (blog) http://fallibleblogma.com/index.php/quote-of-the-
   day-do-it-anyway

10. Rich Mullins, Rich Mullins:
    Never Picture Perfect (©1989 Reunion Records)

11. Maya Angelou, *Quote by Maya Angelou: I've learned that people will forget what you ...* http://www.goodreads.com/quotes/5934-i-ve-learned-that-people-will-forget-what-you-said-people

12. Tom Frye and Jeremy Casella, Frye Family Band: *Under Indiana Lights* (©2011 Oubache Music/ASCAP)

13. Brennan Manning, *Abba's Child: The Cry of the Heart for Intimate Belonging* (Colorado Springs: NavPress, 1994), 105

14. J.R.R. Tolkien, *Lord of the Rings: Fellowship of the Rings*, (Great Britain: HarperCollinsPublishers, 1994), 74.

15. Tom Frye and Jeremy Casella, Frye Family Band: *Under Indiana Lights* (©2011 Oubache Music/ASCAP)

16. Mitch McVicker, Mitch McVicker: Chasing the Horizon (©2000 Out of the Box Records)

17. Rich Mullins, Rich Mullins: *Pictures in the Sky* (©1987 Reunion Records)

18. *Insight for Living.* http://www.insight.org/broadcast/

19. Vance Christie, *Hudson Taylor: Founder, China Inland Mission*, (Urichsville, Ohio Barbour Publishing, Inc., 1999) 175–176

20. Rich Mullins, Rich Mullins: *Pictures in the Sky* (©1987 Reunion Records)

21. *Family Affair.* Don Fedderson and Edmund L. Hartmann (creators) CBS 1966–1971

22. Tom Petty, Tom Petty and the Heartbreakers: *Hard Promises* (©1981 Backstreet Records)

23. Fluid Drive Media, "Advertising: How many marketing messages do we see in a day?" *Advertising* (blog) http://www.fluiddrivemedia.com/advertising/marketing-messages/

24. Nathaniel Hawthorne, *The Scarlet Letter*, (Boston: Ticknor, Reed & Fields, 1850)

25. Beth Moore, *Breaking Free: Discover the Victory of Total Surrender*, (Nashville: B&H Publishing Group, ©2000 Beth Moore, Paper Trade Edition ©2007 Beth Moore), 161.

26. G.K. Chesterton, *Quote by G.K. Chesterton: To love means loving the unlovable. To forgive ...* , http://www.goodreads.com/quotes/376714-to-love-means-loving-the-unlovable-to-forgive-means-pardoning

27. Rich Mullins and Steve Cudworth, Rich Mullins: *Winds of Heaven, Stuff of Earth* (©1988 Reunion Records)

28. Andy Gullahorn, Andy Gullahorn:
    The Law of Gravity (©2009 St. Jerome Music)

29. Tony Campolo, *Carpe Diem*,
    (Nashville, W Publishing Group, 1994), 121–122

30. Rich Stearns, *A Hole in our Gospel*,
    (Nashville: Thomas Nelson Inc., 2009) 186–188

31. Tom Frye and Jeremy Casella, Frye Family Band:
    Under Indiana Lights (©2011 Oubache Music/ASCAP)

32. *Second Hand Lions*. Tim McCanlies (writer/director).
    New Line Productions 2003

Notes

The Fryes are available for speaking engagements, worship services, concerts and Family to Family events.

For booking inquiries, visit:
FamilyFirstMinistries.net
or email info@fryefamilyband.net

On the web:

FamilyFirstMinistries.net
FryeFamilyBand.net

Facebook:

facebook.com/tomfryemusic
facebook.com/fryefamilyband

Twitter:

twitter.com/fryefamilyband

Look for the new EP
Alive for the First Time
available from the Frye Family Band
Summer 2013

Additional albums available from the Fryes:
Under Indiana Lights
Frye Family Band

Songs of a Wilderness Traveler
Tom Frye

Hope is Alive
Tom Frye